TORQUEMADA AND ESMERALDA

Two Short Plays by Victor Hugo

BY

VICTOR HUGO

Fredonia Books
Amsterdam, The Netherlands

Torquemada and Esmeralda:
Two Short Plays by Victor Hugo

by
Victor Hugo

ISBN: 1-58963-480-2

Copyright © 2001 by Fredonia Books

Fredonia Books
Amsterdam, The Netherlands
http://www.fredoniabooks.com

All rights reserved, including the right to reproduce this book, or portions thereof, in any form.

In order to make original editions of historical works available to scholars at an economical price, this facsimile of the original edition is reproduced from the best available copy and has been digitally enhanced to improve legibility, but the text remains unaltered to retain historical authenticity.

TORQUEMADA

PART I.

DRAMATIS PERSONÆ

TORQUEMADA.
DON SANCHO DE SALINAS.
DONNA ROSE D'ORTHEZ.
GIL, MARQUIS DE FUENTEL.
FERDINAND, KING.
ALEXANDER IV., POPE.
FRANCIS DE PAULA.
GUCHO, *buffoon*.
THE PRIOR.
THE BISHOP OF SEO D'URGEL.

Monks. Soldiers

TORQUEMADA.

ACT I.

THE IN PACE.

SCENE. — *Catalonia Mountains, on the border. The Laterran Monastery, an Augustinian convent belonging to the observance of Saint Ruf.*

The old convent cemetery, looking wild and uncared for. It is the month of April in the south of Europe. There are flowers, and the sun shines brightly. Crosses and tombs scattered along the turf and under the trees. The soil is broken up with graves. In the background, the wall enclosing the monastery, very high, but falling into ruin. It is split by a wide gap reaching to the ground, and the country is seen in the distance. In an angle near a part of the wall, an iron cross planted above a grave.

Another very high cross, with the mystic triangle, gilt, is placed on the summit of a stone pedestal, and commands the cemetery.

In the fore-ground, close to the soil, a square opening, encircled by flat stones on a level with the grass. Beside it is seen a long slab apparently intended to close the opening at need. In the opening the first steps of a narrow stone staircase are distinguished, which descends and is lost in a vault. It is a sepulchre from which the cover has been taken, allowing the interior to be seen. The slab close by is the cover.

On the rising of the curtain, THE PRIOR *of the convent, in the Augustinian habit, is on the scene. A monk is passing silently across the back-ground. He is old, and clad in the Dominican robe. He walks slowly, bending the knee before every cross he meets, and disappears.* THE PRIOR *is alone.*

SCENE I.

[THE PRIOR *of the convent, then* A MAN. THE PRIOR, *bald, with a tonsure of grey hair, white beard, and drugget robe. He examines the wall, and moves pensively among the tombs.*

THE PRIOR.

A convent badly kept! A tangled waste
Of briar and brush, — such desolation Time,
Old renegade, in holy places works.
            [*He examines the breach in the wall.*
Through yonder gap a novice might get free.
'T would seem as if, tired of its lengthened ward,
This rampart now refuses further service.
Ah, well! in this its ruin but depicts
Our crumbling rights that also suffer blight, —
Our rights, through which a yawning gap is forced.
The branch divine grows withered in the hand
That erst received it green. Our sluggard popes
Shrink from the battle's brunt. To-day, alas!
The cloister has no sanctity for princes.
Dark as the shadow from the eagle's wings,
They pass above our heads. We meet no more
The reverence deep of old. No charter now
Comes to us as a gift from royal hands.
Lower we ever stoop, — for fear of blows!
Nay more, we are not sure but that our halls
Are nests where courtiers hatch their vile intrigues.
To bring their princelets up they force us too,
Hid from the gaze of men, both boys and girls;
Bastards, perhaps, — who knows? — and we obey.
      [*He pauses in front of the entrance to the vault.*

We are the victims of the very courts
That meet within our walls, and we alone.
                        [*He stands gazing on the wall.*
And, like ourselves, our ancient fabric totters.
Christ bleeds; we grope in shadow. All our steps
Are set in shame and darkness —
[A MAN *enters the breach, muffled in a cloak, with his hat pulled down over his eyes. He stops on reaching the pile of stones in the breach.* THE PRIOR *perceives him.*

THE PRIOR.
                        Man, begone!

THE MAN.
No.

THE PRIOR.
  Get thee hence! This is a graveyard, clown.

THE MAN.
Eh, well, what then?

THE PRIOR.
         A famous cloister.

THE MAN.
                            Bah!

THE PRIOR.
No one comes hither save the monks alone,
When daylight shines; and in the night, the dead,
Wrapped in their winding-sheets. Whoever else
Dares to intrude, no mercy need expect, —
If duke, the axe; if commoner, the cord.
The monks alone have right of entrance here.
Beware! — (*with a haughty smile*).
                Unless, perchance, thou art the King.

THE MAN.
I am.

THE PRIOR.
You are the King!

THE MAN.
Yes, so men call me.

THE PRIOR.
How prove you this?

THE MAN.
Why, thus.

[*He makes a sign. A troop of soldiers appears at the breach.* THE KING *points to* THE PRIOR.

Hang me that man.

[*The Soldiers enter and surround* THE PRIOR. *Enter with them* THE MARQUIS DE FUENTEL *and* GUCHO.

THE MARQUIS DE FUENTEL *with a grey beard, dressed in the rich costume of a Knight of Alcantara.* GUCHO, *the dwarf, dressed in black, with cap and bells. He holds two bawbles with both hands, one in gold in the form of a man, the other in copper in the form of a woman.*

SCENE II.

THE PRIOR, THE KING, THE MARQUIS DE FUENTEL, GUCHO, *escort of* THE KING.

THE PRIOR (*falling on his knees*).
Pardon, my liege!

THE KING.
I grant it on condition.
What are you in this convent?

THE PRIOR.
Prior.

THE KING.
                                           Take heed.
Inform me fully on what passes here.
Speak falsely and the gibbet is your doom;
If true your words, your pardon stands; and now,
Marquis, before beginning, let us pray.
[*He flings his cloak to a lackey, behind, and appears in the undress habit of Alcantara. A large rosary hangs from his girdle. He recites the rosary for some minutes in silence, and then turns again to* THE MARQUIS.
The Queen is far from here. I feel alive.
To be alone's delicious. Still, to be
A widower would be better yet. The thought
Moves me to laughter.

    GUCHO (*on the ground, doubled up at a corner of a tomb with the two bawbles in his arms*).
                          And the wide world weeps.

               THE KING (*to* THE MARQUIS).
It is my will that you should know the motives
That urge me to examine for myself
This cloister's mode of living. Follow me.
[*He makes a sign to* THE MARQUIS *to come a little aside, near the tomb where* GUCHO *has squatted.*

                     THE MARQUIS.
I hear my sovereign.
                          GUCHO (*aside*).
                               And I hear the wind
That murmurs high above the things you do.

                THE KING (*to* THE MARQUIS).
I want your guidance in some secret things.

GUCHO (*aside*).
What is it to me! While I can eat and sleep
Why, all is well!

THE MARQUIS (*to* THE KING).
Shall we send Gucho hence?

THE KING.
No need. He understands us not. (*To* GUCHO.)
Lie there.
[GUCHO *makes himself as small as he can in the shadow of* THE KING, *who approaches* THE MARQUIS.
Marquis, my love for woman has no bounds;
That you are vicious also pleases me, —
Or were. With age you have religious grown.
And, Marquis, that is well. 'T is faith alone
Gives man his value and blots out his stains.
[*He makes the sign of the cross.*

THE MARQUIS.
The convent that your Majesty inspects
Two patrons has, one living at Cahors,
And one at Ghent.

THE KING.
If rumour tells the truth,
You have not been a stranger to intrigues,
Nor are you now; and pretty women have
In by-gone days run danger for your sake.
'T is said that you were once a charming page, —
A fact that now may seem impossible.
But why? The morning smiles for all, and then
The day grows dark; it is the general law.
You have not heard a story that is told
Of a court lackey who might have been **you**?
You never called yourself Gorvona?

THE MARQUIS.
                    Never!
Why should I do so?
            THE KING.
            Oh, they say it was
To mask your craft, and guide and help you on
To win a princess's favours.

            THE MARQUIS.
                    No, 't is false!

            THE KING.
The story I have heard entire concerns
A stupid King to whom you gave an heir;
But in what land it happened, none agree.
A fable very likely.

            THE MARQUIS.
            Sire, it is.
You made me Count, and so they wish me harm.

            THE KING.
Not without cause. But whether true or false
What men may say of you, as for myself
I have for law to stand supreme above
All that the minds of men can body forth.
Nothing can touch me, for I am the King!
The vileness of the source from which you sprung,
Your fellowship with lackeys and buffoons,
Your tortuous windings, writhings in the dark,
Are what I like. No one can tell the name
Your father bore, — not even yourself. And I
Admire the skill of him who braves the eyes
Of all the world, yet hides himself from all.
For life like yours, so vagrant and enslaved,
A basilisk's cave or nest of cormorant

TORQUEMADA.

Would seem a fitting starting-point. Yet I
Have made you Count, a grandee of Castile,
And Marquis, — honours though ill-got well-won.
Cunning and force you use with equal skill.
You would out-talk a council of the Church,
Or, failing, scatter it, though the devil was there.
You can be daring, and yet full of wiles;
And, formed to crawl, you boldly front the storm.
Nay, for some giddy whim you'd run a risk,
And grasp the sword in your old age again.
The evil you advise you would not do.
Of nothing innocent, of nothing guilty, —
Such is your nature, Count; and I believe
You can do anything, — ay, even love,
And that sincerely. First you turned, they say,
From lackey to brigand, to courtier next.
Smiling I watch your crafty stratagems.
To view a reptile wind and crawl along
Yields me a sort of pleasure. So your schemes,
Unwound in thoughtful silence, filaments
That float awhile and then are lost in night,
Your talents, fortunes, wit, and baseness, — all
Combine to form a something sinister,
Strange, and disgusting which I like to use.

THE MARQUIS.

My liege, the Tagus, Ebro, Guadalquivir
You hold in fee; and Naples now obeys
Your sovereign will as freely as Castile.
The King of France lies vanquished in the lists;
Already Africa has felt your power;
And where the sun rises above Algiers
The lengthening shadow of my King extends.
Your birthplace, Sos, close bordering on Navarre,
Gives you some right to rule that kingdom, which

You seized while sleeping in your cradle. Kings
Are never born but that some wonder happens.
Although a Catholic king you placed your foot
Upon the Church, within whose breast ferment
Some germs republican; and, thanks to you,
Before the King the sovereign pontiff trembles,
Before your towers his belfries hold their peace.
From Etna to the Ganges wave your flags.
Gonzalo of Cordova leads your troops;
And yet without his aid you win great battles.
You swayed kings like a greybeard, in your teens;
And when you send some priest to row your galleys,
Rome, stammering, unsays her wrathful curse.
Oh, conqueror of Toro! King! I feel
How impotent the words I utter are!
You are so great, and I so very small.
I am devoted to you, sire —

THE KING.
    'T is false.
THE MARQUIS.
My liege —

THE KING.
   Oh, bore me not with your devotion!
To you I am unknown; while you to me
Are not quite clear. Meanwhile we play our parts, —
I, of good prince, and you, of honest man.
At heart we really detest each other.
I loathe the lackey, you abhor the king.
You would assassinate me if you could;
And I some day, perhaps, shall have your head.
Till then we are good friends —
    [THE MARQUIS *opens his mouth to protest*
        A truce to words,
My courtier friend. I hate you; you hate me.

In me lies darkness, black desires in you.
Each keeps his own abyss within himself.
We pierce each other somewhat. Windows dim
Allow some knowledge of our evil hearts.
Your love, old traitor, your devotedness,
Excite my laughter. But until the day
You can no longer from my pouch draw gold,
And while your interest, the surest bond,
Brings us together, I will seek your aid,
Knowing full well the wickeder you are
The better service you can render me.
Down with your mask and mine! It is my will
To speak the truth. An insult none would dare
To offer me, I, Marquis, offer all.
At least I can be frank when arrant knaves
Are witness to my words. If trembling truth
Flies from the prince's ear, his mouth will hold her.
And you shall prove by your base, faltering tongue
Your King is candid, and his lackey lies.
Now let us talk —

   THE MARQUIS.
   But —

   THE KING.
       Ah, what bondage 't is
To be a king! And to be flushed with youth,
On fire with riot and tumultuous hate,
Hot-headed, mocking, boiling with ardent life,
A hurricane of passions at the heart,
To be a blending dark of blood and fire
And powder, and with sudden whims that match
The flashes of the thunder-bolt; to wish
To make a trial of all things in life,
All things to sully and all things to seize;
To thirst for woman, hunger after pleasure;

To see no virgin, no forbidden thing,
Without the fell desire of snapping at it!
To feel oneself a man from head to heel,
And after all, in some magnificent night,
To listen pallid to a voice that cries
With ceaseless repetition: "Be a phantom!"
To be not even a king, alas! — to be
A kingdom! and to feel that in yourself
A hideous medley formed of states and towns
Usurps the place your instincts, will, desires,
Should fill, while towers and provinces and walls
Lie crossing one another in your bowels!
To gaze upon the map and say, "'T is I;
You see me there! Girona is my heel,
Alcala is my head:" and to behold
An appetite that takes an empire's shape
Grow daily in my soul; to feel the flow
Of mighty streams across me, and the seas
That hem you in within their bitter folds;
To bear the stifling torture of the flame
The waves conceal, and have your gloomy soul
Infiltered by the world. And then my wife, —
A monster nothing moves, whose slave I am.
In sombre glare, because she is so high,
We live our lonely lives; and when together,
We are at once omnipotent and sad,
Feeling a chill whene'er we touch each other.
God on some dun and tragic height has placed,
Above the Algarves, Jaen, Arragon,
The Castiles, Burgos, and Leon, two worms
Two masks, two nullities, — a king and queen.
The one is terror, and the other fear.
Ah, yes, it would be sweet to be a king,
If that, in sooth, the tyrant did not feel
The burthen of the tyranny himself!

But to be always on our guard, and eye
Each other with a look that masks the soul, —
Two dumb and pallid statues, both remote
Alike from tears and smiles! Urraca lives
In her again, again in me Alonzo;
A man of stone beside a wife of bronze!
The people, prostrate, grovel at our feet
In awe-struck adoration; and yet we,
The while their benedictions mount from earth,
Feel in ourselves that we are both accursed.
The incense tremulous ascends and forms
A shadow, in which indistinctly blend
The idols, Ferdinand and Isabel.
The brightness of our twin thrones is confused.
We see each other vaguely through a mist;
And when we speak, the grave unbars its door.
I am not very sure she is not dead.
She is a tyrant, and not less a corpse,
And I must freeze her when our crossing hands
Do clasp a mutual sceptre, as if God
Did with a fillet bind a mummy's hand
Entwined with fingers of a skeleton!
And yet for all I live! That stilted ghost
Is not my real self. Oh, no! oh, no!
So when I can, I flee this crushing greatness, —
Escape, and get outside the royal skin,
And, like a dragon that uncoils itself
And rears its crest towards the sun, I feel
The monstrous upgrowth of awakening life.
Mad as the tempest or the hurricane
With frenzy, I, grim captive of a throne,
Break loose, and shaking off the yoke, I rush
In wild intoxication through all things,
And try all fortunes, good and bad alike;
My single aim, to be the animal.

I trample on my royal mantle, and
My soul expands until her bounds extend
To vices, songs, and orgies of the night,
I view my growing lusts and sprouting nails, —
I who at once am prisoner, martyr, king.
A bishop's crosier and a woman's shame
Lash me alike to madness, and I am
Ferocious and infuriate and gay.
The man that seethes within me, flame and slime,
By changing to a demon gets revenge
For being once the spectre that he was!
[*Pensive.*] And yet, but for a moment free, to-morrow
Again a ghost and shadow I become!
[*To* THE MARQUIS.] Colossuses by atoms are not
    pierced,
And so thou dost not understand why I
Do thus unblushingly show forth myself
Before the eyes of men. But I know well
That all to whom I so unfold myself
Tremble the more, the more I play the cynic;
And 't is my joy, while laughing in their midst,
By baring to their gaze my shameless soul,
To render them even viler than they are.
And I, who was but King, feel I am free
When I discard all reverence and shame.
Thou dost not understand me, and dost grow
More terrified. 'T is well. When my cold gaze
Meets thine to-morrow, thou wilt trembling stand,
And doubt, and think that it was sure a dream,
This drunkness into which I plunge myself
Before thee now, this seething caldron where
My past, my rank and power flame up and boil
Beneath thine eyes, and which I shall leave — frozen!
                    [*He takes his chaplet again.*
And now to end our prayers.

GUCHO (*aside, looking slyly at* THE KING).
                    Well done! Yes, pray!

                    THE KING.
And then this monk I'll question.

            GUCHO (*watching him as he prays, aside*).
                                Mummery!
That is the style in which this King will end!
Knavish and harsh, he has no faith in aught;
And still — such chaos is his gloomy soul! —
He says a pater and becomes a fool.
At such a moment to the Pope he yields,
And venerates a council. Though he give
Some hard knocks to the priest, he fears him still;
He feels he is but dust beneath the feet
Of some proud monk like yonder passer-by.
                    [*Making the sign of the cross.*
Amen! He is a shameless knave, a liar,
A crafty, cruel wretch, obscene and godless,
But Catholic! a name — worse come to worst! —
By which he will be later known.
[THE KING *again hangs his rosary to his belt and makes a sign to* THE PRIOR *to approach.*

                    THE KING (*to* THE PRIOR).
                                Come here.
[THE PRIOR *advances, his hand crossed on his breast and his eyes bent on the ground.*
If by ill luck thy answers miss the truth,
And are not frank and full, look to thyself!
                                [THE PRIOR *bows.*
The truth, Beware!
[*A few moments before this, the monk, clad in the garb of a Dominican, has re-appeared at the back of the thea-*

tre. He walks with bent head, regardless of everything, and solely engaged in saluting all the crosses of the tombs before which he passes. He seems to be muttering prayers. He is noticed by THE KING, *who points him out to* THE PRIOR.

And first, who is that monk
With haggard eyes, not clad like thee, who kneels
Each time he meets a cross?

THE PRIOR.

He is insane.

THE KING.

How pale he looks!

THE PRIOR.

With fast and watching he
Wears out his strength. He speaks aloud, and walks
Bare-headed in the sun, and raves and rants.
He has a craze about confronting popes,
And telling them on bended knee their duty.
We must be silent when he passes by.
He is not of our order, and is here
Under our watch and ward; for thus all priests
Are shut up in our convents who may be
Too restless or too learned, dreamers who
Might preach some doctrine which our Spanish church
Disowns.

THE KING.

What is the nature of his madness?

THE PRIOR.

He thinks his eyes see fire, the devil, and hell.
He's but a short time here.

THE KING.

He's old.

THE PRIOR.
                                        He is,
And has, I fancy, not much time to live.
[*The monk passes and disappears without seeing anybody*

          GUCHO (*gazing at his bawbles, aside*).
I have two bawbles. One is gold and one
Is copper; Evil one is called, and Good
The other. I love both with equal love.
I have no aim.   [*He observes the turf on the graves.*
              Down yonder there are flowers,
And yonder withered leaves.

               THE KING (*to* THE PRIOR).
                        The discipline
That ought to guide your convents, monk, has grown
Exceeding lax.
                THE PRIOR.
          My liege —

                THE KING.
                    And it is said
That women are no strangers in your cloisters.

                THE PRIOR.
We're neighbour to a convent in which dwell
The Ursulines. They are our flock; we are —

                THE KING.
The goats, no doubt, that guard the sheep.

               THE PRIOR (*bowing*).
                                   My liege —
          GUCHO (*aside*).
Each women's convent has for confessors
The monks that live close by, who make the sin,

And then absolve it; reigning o'er these hearts,
They rob them of their virtue, then restore
Their innocence.   A pleasant miracle!

THE PRIOR.
The sons of Levi, King, and Sion's daughters —

THE KING.
Lived happily together.   Still I will
Be rigorous, and Rome shall know —

THE PRIOR (*bowing*).
My liege!
GUCHO (*aside*).
When at the cloister's gate, where Jesus reigns
No longer, little Cupid comes to knock,
Pope Sixtus, who two children had, can't scold
If they should set the door ajar.

THE KING (*to* THE PRIOR).
And Rome
Stands ready to inflict a chastisement
For which the times seem ripe.
   [*Looking fixedly at* THE PRIOR.]   Within your walls
At present dwells the Bishop of Urgel, —
I have been warned 't is so, —
   [THE PRIOR *bends his head.*]   With power entire
To punish.

THE PRIOR (*with a new reverence*).
But, my liege, his power extends
To dogma only, and to errors which
Require repression, — nothing more than this.

THE MARQUIS (*in a low tone to* THE KING).
Your eyes see far, my liege.

THE KING (*in a low tone to* THE MARQUIS).
I chose to see.
[*The eyes of* THE KING *are arrested by the subterranean vault, open at some steps from him.*
Monk, what is this?

THE PRIOR.
It is an open tomb.

THE KING.
An open tomb!

THE PRIOR.
It is, my liege.

THE KING.
For whom?

THE PRIOR.
None know but God the moment when man falls.

THE KING.
Whose tomb is this?
[THE PRIOR *keeps silent.* THE KING *becomes urgent.*
Tell me, at once, I say.

THE PRIOR.
I know not. It awaits [*after a silence*], perhaps, myself;
Perhaps it waits for you.

THE MARQUIS (*in* THE KING'S *ear*).
When in a cloister
'T is felt some monk has reached a higher level,
Whether in good or evil, than his fellows,
He is suppressed.

THE KING (*in a low tone*).
	It proves their sense, in **truth,**
To kill in such a case.

THE MARQUIS.
		Oh, no! The Church
Recoils from bloodshed. He is buried merely.

THE KING.
I understand.

THE MARQUIS.
	In this secluded spot,
Cry out! Why, none will hear. Resist! 'T is vain.
No helper will be nigh.
[*Showing the hole, where a staircase is distinguished, and
   then the flag close to it.*
			The man is pushed
Down step by step until he reach the bottom.
And when he touches that, yon stone is placed
Above his head, and night forever fills
His eyelids, hiding from him woods and skies,
And men and waters. Living —

THE KING.
				He is dead.
The thing is simple, truly.

THE MARQUIS.
			If he likes,
He dies. The Church has not shed blood.
	[*A nod of approval on the part of* THE KING

THE KING (*aloud, looking into the garden of the convent*).
					In spite
Of all this monk may say, 't is certain women —

THE PRIOR.
Come not within our walls.

THE KING (*to* THE MARQUIS).
How he does lie!
I see one now!
[*He gazes into the depths of the garden, and continues.*
And by her side a youth,
A charming, beardless boy, all but a child,
Bright-eyed and slender-shaped —

THE PRIOR.
She is, my liege,
A princess.
THE KING.
And the youth?

THE PRIOR.
My liege, a prince.

THE KING (*to* THE MARQUIS, *in a low voice*).
I have done well to come.

THE PRIOR.
The rule *Magnates* —
[*Saluting* THE KING
We are the subjects of Viscount d' Orthez —

THE KING.
And mine as well.

THE PRIOR (*continuing*).
Allows us to receive
One of a princely house.

THE KING.
                    And even two, —
A female and a male.

THE PRIOR (*bowing in the direction to which the finger of*
                    THE KING *points*).
                    She is a countess

THE MARQUIS (*in a low voice to* THE KING).
The King of France is bishop in a land
He does not rule.   The Viscount of Orthez,
Cahors, and Dax resembles him in this;
For, though a layman, yet, as being prince,
He is a cleric, and while battling yonder
Among his subjects, and while crying out:
"Brave troopers, forward!   Forward, men-at-arms!"
He's cardinal-deacon, abbot of this convent.

                    THE KING (*laughing*).
Churchman in Spain, and man of war in France.

THE MARQUIS (*pointing to the two persons whom* THE
                    KING *saw outside the theatre*).
And if yon lusty blade finds here his mate,
The reason is that, for some scheme or other,
Our Viscount placed these hearts among the flowers
And in the shadow, side by side, concealed.

                    THE KING (*seriously*).
Some scheme or other?   No, I see his aim, —
A marriage. [*To* THE PRIOR.] Pray, how long have
    they been here?
                    THE PRIOR.
Since they were children.

THE KING (*to* THE MARQUIS).

                    And have grown up both
Within this stifling priory? [*To* THE PRIOR.] Their
    names?

THE PRIOR.

The one is the infanta Rose d' Orthez.

THE KING.

And the infante.

THE PRIOR.

                Sancho de Salinas.
[THE MARQUIS *starts, and looks eagerly in the direction in
which* THE KING *has perceived the infanta and infante.*

THE KING (*with increasing seriousness*).

Of Burgos he's the heir; she, of Orthez.

THE PRIOR (*making a sign in the affirmative*).

He's rightful lord of lands that even reach
The Tagus.

THE MARQUIS (*aside*).

         Burgos! Sancho de Salinas!
Could this be possible?

THE KING (*to* THE PRIOR).

                Continue. Yes,
All this was planned in secret. Sancho is
My cousin. Still, I thought the eldest branch
Extinct.

THE PRIOR.

        Not so. Don Sancho has been kept
In secret here. He has been sent to us
To be brought up along with Orthez's niece.

THE MARQUIS (*aside*).
And yet I thought them dead. A marvellous
Disclosure this, which I half comprehend.
That boy concealed! It surely must be he!
I feel a sudden rending of the heart.
A wondrous tale, indeed!

THE KING (*to* THE MARQUIS).
                      'T was wise to choose
This lonely convent.

THE PRIOR.
                Soon the Countess, who
To the infante lately pledged her troth,
Shall be his bride. From the same ancestor
They 're both descended, and that ancestor
A saint, whose aid we daily here invoke.
His son, Loup Centulle, was a Gascon duke.
From him came Luke, King of Bigorre; from him,
The King of Barège, John; next after him,
The Viscount Peter; then Gaston the Fifth —

THE KING.
Be brief.

THE PRIOR.
        To-day the reigning Cardinal-Viscount wills
That we, as far as in our power lies,
Shall keep them hidden in our cloisters.

THE MARQUIS (*aside*).
                        Sancho!

THE KING (*pointing to the young man whom he has
    perceived, but who is not seen by the audience*).
A handsome fellow this! Pray, Marquis, look!
[THE MARQUIS *looks in the direction designated by* THE
    KING *with a sort of terrified intentness.*

THE PRIOR (*looking in the same direction*).

He has the right of keeping in his train
A guard of fifty soldiers, all hidalgos,
Commanded by an abbot. When he goes
To church he sits within the altar rails;
Peñacerrada is his capital.
But as it seems, some fatal shadow frowned
Upon his birth. None, sire, save me alone,
Know that he is infante and the heir.
He knows it not himself, and, for like cause,
The infanta Rose is unaware she is
A princess. It is clear that some one's feared.

THE KING.

By heavens! I, the King, might well be wroth
When such a game as this is played.
[*To* THE PRIOR, *always looking outside.*] They wear
A robe of serge like yours.

THE PRIOR.

                   Because they both
Are to the Virgin consecrated, else
We could not keep them in the convent, sire.
They even took their vows as novices
In presence of the chapter.

THE KING.

            Ah! Why, then,
He's very near a monk, and she a nun!

THE PRIOR.

Yes, but they shall have dispensations such
As princes have, and so they can be married.

THE KING (*to* THE MARQUIS).
Then I, the wolf, enter the sheepfold, and
Can spoil it all.   [*Pensive, aside.*]   Look to it, Cardinal!
So thou wouldst trick me, aged demon, who
Hast caused these angels to grow up together!
Adore each other, children, tenderly!
The plot against me I shall surely shape
To my good uses.   Yes!   Let Rose and Sancho
In wedlock join!   That will subserve my turn.
Thou wilt, my Viscount, by a marriage that
Unites my cousin to thy niece, rob me
Of Burgos through Salinas?   It is well.
I yield compliance.   Now our rights are equal.
But, like thyself, I do not care to part
With what is mine.   And I, by Orthez, mean
To take from thee Navarre   Through her I hold thee,
As thou dost me through him.   So therefore let
This marriage be performed.   I am well pleased
To-day the bridal, the assault to-morrow!   [*Looking outside.*
She is a lovely girl!   [*Pensive.*]   The way to reign
Triumphant is to use the secret springs
Your enemy employs, for your own weal,
And use them in a careless, drowsy fashion.
An intrigue, thwarted thus, becomes your servant.
The arm would slay you turns aside and fails.
The stupid dagger strikes the place you wish,
And your assassin changes to your slave.
                              [*Again gazing outside.*
What are they saying?   I must listen.
[*He proceeds to the back of the theatre and disappears
   among the trees.*

   GUCHO (*aside, looking at* THE KING *as he goes out*).
                                             Spy!
[*As soon as* THE KING *has left*, THE MARQUIS *beckons imperiously to* THE PRIOR *to draw near him.*

SCENE III.

The same, except THE KING; THE MARQUIS, THE PRIOR *who are supposed to be inaudible to the other performers. They are at the front of the stage.*

THE MARQUIS.
Come hither, priest!

THE PRIOR (*approaching submissively*).
My humble service.
[*He makes a profound reverence to* THE MARQUIS

THE MARQUIS.
           Thou
Hast not informed the King of all.

THE PRIOR.
          The Lord
Alone is master, and whate'er the priest
May in confession learn, he must not tell.

THE MARQUIS.
A fiction that. Has it not been declared
By Paul the Second that in cases grave
All things may be revealed? If thou dost dare
To brave my wrath, then woe to thee, O monk!

THE PRIOR.
But swear you will be secret if I yield.

THE MARQUIS.
I swear it; nay, I will do better still;
A golden head-dress worth a hundred marks

I promise I'll to thy madonna give,
And six huge silver candelabra which
Of equal value are.
THE PRIOR.
You shall know all.
What time, my lord, both you and I were young,
The Princess, Donna Sancha of Portugal,
For whom our prayers are offered every fast,
Gave to her wedded lord, the King of Burgos,
An heir whose father was the page, Gorvona.
The King, who held in great esteem his wife,
Believed the child his own, and so of right
This bastard did become legitimate,
Succeeded to the crown and all its powers
Then married, died, and left an only son,
Who met, it was believed, a sudden death
While yet a child. But no, he was, in truth,
Abducted by the Cardinal-Viscount, who
Had seized and hidden in his fief of Bearn
The little king, Don Sancho.

THE MARQUIS (*aside*).
Yes, 't is clear.
I guessed aright.
   [*Gazing outside while* THE PRIOR *is muttering prayers*
It is my child! the son
Of mine own son! Great God! I scarcely dare
Believe it yet. I feel awake within
My bosom something I knew not was there, —
A heart! O sacred lightning flash! O swift,
Subduing shock! I who once hated, love!
My son! my son! Oh, I am drunk with joy!
A joy that for the present, almost kills me.
O blest release! Now I have burst my bonds!
I lived for evil; I will live for good.

My blackened conscience prowled as does the wolf.
I thought I had lost all, and have found all!
I am a father, grandsire! O my God!
And from below I can henceforward look
With smiles upon the radiant heights above,
Can cast a furtive glance toward the peak
On which shall grow this glorious lily, sprung
From out my dunghill, and say, "'T is my son!"
And oh, to live anew myself! I feel
This child, enrobed in all his radiance, comes
Into the turbid mist that girds me round,
And that his fresh young soul the owner is
Of this vile withered heart, so that there is
Within myself a watchful innocence
That I can trust for guidance and support.
I am another man, and weep and pray,
And on my sinful night there breaks the dawn!
This light is mine! this artless boy is mine!
Art thou at last, then, merciful, O God!
Thou dark, unknown existence? Even I,
The prompter of this King who sets his feet
Upon his victims; I, the light by which
His foulness walks; I, courtier of his crimes,
Know that a soft hand wipes away my stains.
Yes, I, his hideous henchman, breathe at last,
And raise my head again — alas! weighed down
By dire remorse! — Yes, I can breath again,
Uncursed of God! I am no more alone;
I live, I love! O dazzling thought! Alas!
He has but me, and I have only him.
What gulfs surround him! What unnumbered snares!
But I shall watch. [*Pensive.*]. For him the light, for me
The gloom. The cloak in which I wrap myself
Must not be cast aside. A faint surmise
As to the father would destroy the son.

[*He returns to* THE PRIOR.

THE PRIOR (*in a low voice*).
You promised secrecy, my lord.

THE MARQUIS.
                    The pledge,
Be sure, I'll keep. When does Don Sancho quit
His refuge here?

THE PRIOR.
                    The child, who was thought dead,
Is now a man. My lord, the Cardinal
Thinks to make use of him, and will, when he
Is husband of his niece, declare him king,
And prince and highness.
[*He casts a look behind.* THE KING *appears at the back.*
            Lo! the King!

THE MARQUIS.
                        The King!
            [*Aside, speaking to himself.*
Old man, take care to screen from this King's eyes
The heart unhoped for that has flowered in thee.

THE PRIOR (*in a low voice*).
Protect us. And God grant that nothing here
Excite his anger!

THE MARQUIS (*aside*).
                Now, old mummer, now,
Resume thy craven mask, insensible
Alike to insult, hatred, and affront,
And call back to thy lips that abject smile.

THE PRIOR.
You pledged, my lord, the greatest secrecy.

THE MARQUIS (*aside*).

Yes, yes, I must! [*To* THE PRIOR.] You need not fear.
Be calm.

SCENE IV.

The same. THE KING.

THE KING (*aside*).

To spy half-open hearts amuses me.
[*He looks back in the direction from which he has entered.*
[*To* THE MARQUIS.] They're yonder. Now we leave.

THE MARQUIS.

On what have you,
Their lord and king, resolved?

THE KING.

To make them happy.
I wish them married.

THE MARQUIS.

'T is deep policy.

THE KING.

Spain, stone by stone, and step by step's a-building.
This marriage runs concordant with my plans.
The Cardinal d' Orthez shall have my help,
His wish shall be fulfilled; and, Marquis, I
Shall have Dax and Bayonne a little after.

THE MARQUIS (*aside*).

O fierce and gloomy heart of mine, rejoice!
My child shall be a king!

[*At a sign from* THE KING *the escort and retinue all leave by the breach.* THE PRIOR *approaches and salutes* THE KING, *his arms crossed on his breast.*

THE KING (*to* THE PRIOR).
Monk, I have not come here —

THE PRIOR (*bowing*).
My liege

THE KING.
And thou
Hast never seen me.

THE PRIOR.
Poor, the humble monk,
And naked has —

THE KING.
I shall take care to watch
The doings in this convent.

THE PRIOR.
Where you 'll see
That in its walls your Grace's wishes meet
With prompt obedience ever. [*Aside.*] May a curse
Cleave to thee, King!

THE KING.
Your chief resides in France.

THE PRIOR.
He does, my liege.

THE KING.
The bishop of Urgel
Is here at present.

THE PRIOR.
Yes, we have the honour
To lodge a bishop on his pastoral tour.

THE KING.
He must know naught of what has taken place.
[DON SANCHO *and* DONNA ROSE *are seen at the back of the theatre. They have not perceived anything of what has occurred.* THE KING *points them out to* THE MARQUIS, *and proceeds towards the breach.*
[*To* THE MARQUIS.] Come quick! [*To* THE PRIOR.] If thy intention is to live,
Be silent. [*To* THE MARQUIS.] Come!
[THE KING *goes out,* GUCHO *follows.*

THE MARQUIS (*gazing on* DON SANCHO).
My sweet and lovely child!

SCENE V.

DON SANCHO, DONNA ROSE. DON SANCHO *and* DONNA ROSE, *both dressed as novices, he in a white soutane, she in a veil, are running and playing among the trees. She is sixteen, he seventeen. They are chasing and flying from each other. Laughter and gaiety.* ROSE *tries to catch the butterflies.* SANCHO *gathers flowers, and is arranging a nosegay which he holds in his hand.*

DONNA ROSE.
Come this way! Look, 't is full of butterflies.

DON SANCHO.
The roses please me best.
[*He gathers some wild roses and adds them to his nosegay while looking around him.*
                       Oh, I am thrilled
With rapture at the sight of such sweet things!

DONNA ROSE (*admiring a butterfly*).
See yonder one that flies among the reeds!

DON SANCHO.

With perfumes and with life all things are rife!

DONNA ROSE.

Come, let us share. For you the flowers; for me
The butterflies.

DON SANCHO (*his eyes turned towards the heavens*).
The universe is filled
With something strange of tenderness and grace.
[*He continues to gather flowers for his nosegay while
DONNA ROSE is running after the butterflies. He gazes
after her earnestly.*
Rose!

DONNA ROSE (*turning and looking at the flowers he has
in his hand*).
Sir! For whom do you intend these flowers?

DON SANCHO.

Well, guess.

DONNA ROSE.

For me.
[*She returns to the butterflies, and tries to catch them.
They escape her. She is vexed and speaks to them.*
I think you pretty, yet
You fly away. Why so?

DON SANCHO.

They'll lose, dear Rose,
Their colours if you touch them.
[*Musing, and gazing on the butterflies as they flit about.*

                                One might think
He gazed on wandering kisses seeking mouths.

DONNA ROSE.
They find them, too, — the flowers.

DON SANCHO.
                                Then, my Rose,
Since your 're a flower —
   [*He clasps her in his arm. She struggles; he kisses her.*

DONNA ROSE.
                    Stop, sir; 't is very wrong!

DON SANCHO.
But since we shall be married —
[DONNA ROSE *follows a butterfly with her eyes. She lies
   in wait for it. It rests on a flower.*

DONNA ROSE.
                    Look, it lights.
I must have this one.   [*She approaches softly*
      [*To* DON SANCHO.]   Come.

DON SANCHO (*following her very closely*).
                                Hush!
[*The lips of* DON SANCHO *meet the lips of* DONNA ROSE;
   the butterfly escapes.

DONNA ROSE.
                            Stupid man!
That don't know how to take a butterfly

DON SANCHO.
But I have ta'en the kiss.

ROSE (*surveying the butterflies returning to the flowers*).
                    How daintily
They place themselves right at their ladies' feet! —
There now! They leave them, little faithless things!
                    [*She gazes on them as they fly.*
Why do they fly so far, and go so high?
What numberless wings are flitting through the air!
[DON SANCHO *comes gently behind her, and embraces her.
    She repulses him.*
A kiss before our marriage! Never, sir.
I will not have it. No.

                    DON SANCHO.
                    Then give it back.

                    DONNA ROSE (*smiling*).
No.
                    DON SANCHO.
    Yes.
                    DONNA ROSE.
            But — Ah! I love thee!
[*They embrace each other, and sit down on a tomb. She
    rests her head on his shoulder. Both, as if in ecstasy,
    follow the butterflies with their eyes.*

                    DON SANCHO.
                                    Oh, how kind
And boundless is this nature which surrounds us!
Give ear, until its meaning I unfold.
From winter's gloomy sky there falls on earth
A pale and chilling winding-sheet; but when
April returns, the flowers bloom again,
The days grow long; and then the happy earth
Rewards the heavens that have protected her
With flakes of snow changed to white butterflies.
High festival is kept where mourning was,

And all the skies are blue, and trembling joy
Takes flight and mounts to God.   Such is the cause
Why from the dark springs forth this rush of wings.
God opens underneath his boundless heaven
The countless hearts of men, and makes them full
Of rapture and of light; and nothing can
Refuse his bounty or disown his sway,
For everything that he has made is good!

DONNA ROSE.

Oh, how I love thee!

DON SANCHO (*passionately*).

Rose!

[*He clasps her in his arms. A butterfly passes.* DONNA ROSE *tears herself from the embrace of* DON SANCHO, *and runs after the butterfly.*

DONNA ROSE.

How beautiful!
Come, come!   We must take this one.   Come!

DON SANCHO.

God strews
The charms of spring around to glad thine eyes.

[*The butterfly settles on a bush.*

DONNA ROSE (*reaching her hand out to seize it*).

Not so much noise.   [*The butterfly flies away*
How wearisome he is!
He's gone again.

[*She follows the butterfly.* DON SANCHO *follows her.*
Among the lilies.

[*The butterfly flits farther.*
Good!
He's in the clematis.

DON SANCHO.
                    Since we were children
Our souls have always lived close to each other,
O my sweet wife!
                    [*The butterfly is farther still.*

DONNA ROSE.
        He sees me!
[*The butterfly is on the wild-rose bush. She tries to seize it,
and stretches out her hand, but draws it back quickly.*
                    Oh, the rose!
The wicked rose has pricked my finger.

DON SANCHO.
                                        Ah!
Those bad, bad roses! That one wants to drink
The blood of angels!
[THE MONK *in the Dominican habit appears under the
trees, among the tombs. He does not see them.* DONNA
ROSE *perceives him.*
                    Ah! look, there again
Is that old monk who has so strange an air!
That man makes me afraid. Pray, come away.
[*They go out in the direction of the clumps of trees.* THE
MONK *advances slowly, as if he saw nothing beyond
himself. The day is beginning to wane.*

SCENE VI.

THE MONK, *alone.*

THE MONK.

Here! — man's corrupted nature, and the woe
Inherited, the princes all defiled

With abject crimes, the sages past all cure,
And lust and pride and foaming blasphemy
And murderous Sennacherib and false
Delilah, heretics, Musarabs, Jews,
Waldenses, Guebers, and those pallid fools,
The curious in algebras and ciphers,
All, all, both great and little, have befouled
Their sign baptismal, groping in the dark,
Denying Jesus, prone to wrongful deeds,
All, all! the pope and king, the bishop, priest!
And there, the infinite and awful fire!
Here, careless man, who lives and eats and sleeps.
And there, the sombre depths of glowing flame!
There, hell! — O human creature desolate!
O life and death! thou dark and twofold plain
On which our fate is staked. To laugh an hour
And afterward to weep forever! Hell!
O horrid vision! Caves, and mountain tops,
And pits of burning coal, and sulphurous peaks.
O thousand-toothed gulf! O yawning mouth!
Infinite guilt beneath the infinite hand
Of its avenger! Joy makes up one half,
And pain the other. And the scorching heat
Ne'er ceases. Hear ye not those screams! "My son!
My mother! Pardon!" The chimera, Hope,
Falls into ashes. Eyes and faces wan
Are lost awhile within the fiery shaft,
And then return to sight. The melted lead
Drops down on living skulls. A spectre world.
It tortures and it suffers; it is roofed
With hideous vaults that form the nether side
Of pitchy graveyards, pierced with points of fire
As heaven with stars at night. A ceiling dire,
In which are yawning caverns here and there.
Through them there falls, as fast as drops of rain,

Eternally a shower of human souls!
They sink into the caldrons' flaming mouths,
In nameless tortures, farther than can reach
God's pardon; night and anguish are their lot.
A dismal wind howls through the gaps, and whirls
The flames unceasing, fed by other flames.
The swollen, blazing lava fills the deep
And hollow portals. Heaven cries out: Never!
And Hell cries back: Forever! All that have,
While on this earth, by vice or idleness,
Made bad use of their time, made one false step
In drunkness, went astray, fell, sinned, or stumbled,
Though 't were but for one moment's space, is there!
O retribution dread! O headlong fall!
Impossible to doubt. What see we yonder,
Before our very eyes? — Hell visible!
Its pestilential breath comes where we stand,
From Belial's hearth there rises to our sky
The pungent, red-hot smoke his caldrons send
Through his dread chimneys, Mount Vesuvius,
And Etna, Stromboli and northern Hecla.
Of what then should we think if not of this?
We have before us yawning 'neath our earth
This mystery that spits forth flame and death.
We can lean over and can gaze within.
We can at night behold the damned afire,
See whirlwinds of them roll along like sparks,
Take flight and then fall back with fire-charred wings.
Alas! for ye no outlet and no flight!
Back! back! Regain your blazing dungeons. Back!
Become again the waves of that black sea
Of fire and chaos. Satan, outcast fell,
Above you laughs! They whirl around in fright,
Those living brands that shoot forth smoke and flame,
A spectacle of dread! — and scatter through

The fixed and limitless extent of space.
The fiery serpents lick their writhing hands;
Oil bites their limbs, and lead and pitch suck up
Their melting flesh. A darkness fathomless
Spreads o'er their heads its huge, tremendous veil
The Infinite through all its hundred sieves
Lets nothing pass but these two awful words:
Forever! Never! — God! O God! who shall
Have pity on them? — I! Yes, I will save
Mankind. Man pardoned is the thought absorbs
My inmost being. In my soul a love
Sublime cries out. By me abyss shall strive
Against abyss. The work that Dominick
Began I shall accomplish. Hell! Ah, Hell!
How shall I make its iron roof sink down?
How shall I on its horrid steep arrest
The fall of man, O Rome! O Jesus Christ! —
The way I've found, a way Saint Paul has shown
The eagle, as he proudly soars aloft,
Sees all things stretch before his dazzled eyes.
To close hell's gates and open heaven again,
What needs the world? The stake. It needs
The searing of hell's fires, the conquest of
Eternity with but a moment's pain;
One lightning flash of suffering annuls
Unnumbered tortures. All the earth afire
Shall quench this sombre hell. A passing hell
That lasts but for an hour shall sweep away
The stake that is eternal. Sin is burned
Along with its vile rag of flesh. The soul
Springs from the flame refulgent, pure as snow;
For water laves the body, fire the soul.
The one is mud, the other light; and fire,
Handmaiden of heaven's chariot, alone
Makes white the soul, of which it is the sister.

To thee, immortal soul! I sacrifice
The body. Could a father hesitate?
Could a fond mother who should see her child
Hang midway 'twixt the holy stake and hell,
Reject the interchange that kills a demon
And makes anew an angel? Yes, I read
Aright the meaning of the word Redemption.
Gomorrha is eternal as is Sion.
No one can bring down from the radiant heaven
A drop of joy to fire-tormented hell.
But God at least permits to save the future!
Man is the prey of hell no more! The torch
August has come to bless. And oh, there is
No time to lose! Alas! the world grows worse;
And Jesus bleeds and dies a second time.
All men are wicked, evil, vowed to ruin.
From hour to hour shoots up some bud of sin
From that dread, fatal tree whose branches God
Drew toward himself, but which Eve bent, alas!
Again to human lips! Amongst us faith
No longer lives. On every side Beghards,
Backsliding Jews, and monks that break their vows,
And nuns that let their hair again grow long;
This one pulls down a cross, that stains a host,
And faith expires beneath its load of error,
As does the lily weighed down by the nettle.
The Pope is on his knees. In front of whom?
Of God? Of man. He is afraid of Cæsar.
Rome soon, subservient to kings, shall be
The serf of Nineveh. Another step,
And all the world is lost. But I am here,
Am here! — and with me bring the antique fervour.
In pensive sadness I am come to breathe
Upon the saving fagots. Earth, I come
To ransom, at the price of flesh, the soul.

I bear salvation and I bear relief.
Glory to God! and happiness to all!
Those rock-bound hearts shall melt. The blaze of stakes
Shall fill the world. I will fling on the winds
The cry profound of Genesis: Light! Light!
And then the splendours of the burning piles
Will shine o'er all. I'll scatter fires abroad,
And flaming brands, and lustrous furnaces,
Until above the cities of the earth
Autos-da-fe shall blaze on every side,
Supreme and active, and diffusing round
Celestial joys! I love the human race!

[*He raises his eyes to heaven in ecstasy, with clasped hands and wide-open mouth. Behind him, from the outskirt of a kind of thicket at the back of the cemetery, issues a monk with his arms crossed on his breast and his hood pulled down over his face. Then, from another point of the copse, another monk, then another. These monks are in the Augustinian habit. They take their stand, silent and motionless, behind the Dominican monk, who does not see them. Other monks arrive successively in the same fashion, singly and in silence, and place themselves beside the first. All have their arms crossed and their hoods lowered, so as to entirely conceal their faces. After some time a semicircle is formed behind* THE DOMINICAN. *This semicircle divides, and a bishop attended by two archdeacons is seen to issue from the trees with cope on back, crosier in hand, and mitre on head. It is* THE BISHOP OF SEO D'URGEL. *He advances slowly, followed by* THE PRIOR, *who, alone of the monks, has the hood raised.* THE BISHOP, *without saying a word, stations himself in the centre of the semicircle of monks, which closes up behind him.* THE DOMINICAN *has seen nothing of all this. The day continues to wane.*

SCENE VII.

THE DOMINICAN, THE BISHOP OF SEO D'URGEL, THE
PRIOR, *monks*.

THE BISHOP.

Be witnesses that I, John, Bishop, am
About to judge, be he or good or bad,
This man now present, and shall question him
Before the judgment. Equity permits
The punishment, but wills that culprits have
Full notice of the charge.

[THE MONK *has turned round. He observes the proceedings with grave attention. He does not seem moved. He fixes his eyes on* THE BISHOP.

What art thou? Say.

THE MONK.

A friar preacher.

THE BISHOP.

And what is thy name?

THE MONK.

Torquemada.

THE BISHOP.

'T is said that yet a child
The demon did possess thee, and that since
Thou 'rt chased by hideous visions. Is this true?

THE MONK.

Realities alone have power o'er me.

THE BISHOP.

All fancies.

THE MONK.
Be content with visions.   I
See God.
[*Fixing his gaze on the mystic gilt triangle on the top of the great cross of the cemetery.*
What will'st thou, Lord, that we should do,
Who are thy priests before the eternal light?
Behold thy simple and most awful law,
And naught but that.   Oh, it is terrible!
But as for me, how can I help it?

THE BISHOP.
Answer.
'T is said that in your thought we doctors all
Delude ourselves who loathe the impious man
As if he were a panther.

THE MONK.
Yes, my lord,
My lords the bishops do delude themselves.

THE BISHOP.
Thou worm of earth!

THE MONK.
The impious should be loved,—
And saved.

THE BISHOP.
'T is said a dogma false wherein
The Lombard Didier had gone astray
Seduces thee, and in thy vain conceit
Thou holdest hell extinguished by the stake;
So that the flame wafts up to heaven the dead.
And for the soul's salvation we must needs
The body burn.

THE MONK.
'T is truth.

THE BISHOP.
An error, monk,
Bewitches thee. The dismal tree of evil
Has error for its root.

THE MONK.
The soul abhors
Its contact with its vile associate,
The body. Burning is the only way
To purify.

THE BISHOP.
A dreadful doctrine.

THE MONK.
No.

THE BISHOP.
And false.

THE MONK.
And true. And by its guidance, I
Intend to rule my acts.

THE BISHOP.
A viper, thou!

THE MONK.
My faith in it is firm. Ah, yes!

THE BISHOP.
Beware,
Unless thou dost retract! I here command
That thou repent of it, and from this time
Cease to believe in such a heresy.

THE MONK.
I cannot lie, and, in all humbleness,
I must persist.

THE BISHOP.
Thou art perverse!

THE MONK.
I have
With me the Council of the Lateran
And Innocent the Third.

THE BISHOP.
If thou art docile,
Thou hast all things within thy reach. But if
Thou turnest rebel, nothing. Come, my son,
Thy error is a treacherous light that can
Spread mischief round From it a schism might spring.
Come, strike thy breast, and say: "I have been wrong."

THE MONK.
I have been right.

THE BISHOP.
Renounce thy doctrine, like
That Bruno of Angers who wished to grow
To greatness and recanted.

THE MONK.
Yes; but I
Wish not to grow to greatness, but to rest
In my own littleness.

THE BISHOP.
Puffed up with pride!

THE MONK.
Not so, my lord, I am inspired by faith.

THE BISHOP.
But what dost thou intend to do?

THE MONK.
         To go
Barefoot to Rome and warn the Holy Father.

THE BISHOP.
'T was he who ordered me to judge thee, dog!

THE MONK.
The barking of the dog awakes the shepherd.
I shall awake the Pope, and he must listen.

THE BISHOP (*to those present, pointing to* THE MONK).
My sons, this man is ruthless.

THE MONK.
        Yes, because
He is compassionate. Saint Paul has said:
"Faith burns through charity."

THE BISHOP.
         Thou dost mistake
The meaning of the text thou wrongly quotest.
Sixtus the Fourth, a pastor whom the world
In reverence holds, wills that the Church should be
Less rigorous, and faith become more mild.
In him with sanctity indulgence dwells,
And he would armour truth with tenderness.
The Inquisition, too, has gentler grown,
And when the Pope uplifts his sacred hand,
It is to bless, not strike. We seldom see
The smoking fagots now.

THE MONK.
                    This laxity
Appalls my soul. The flames of hell expand
And higher rise, the lower grow the flames
That from the stake ascend.

THE BISHOP.
                        Poor darkened soul!
What is, then, thy desire?

THE MONK.
                    To save the world.

THE BISHOP.
But how?

THE MONK.
            By fire.

THE BISHOP.
                    Beware of remedy
So merciless and savage.

THE MONK.
                        The physician
Is not the master of the remedy.

THE BISHOP.
But, say, what dost thou hope?

THE MONK.
                            To triumph if
God aid me.

THE BISHOP.
                    We shall see.
  [*He shows* THE MONK *the opening of the vault*
            Go, enter there.

THE MONK.

But what is that?

THE BISHOP.

Thy tomb.

THE MONK.
                    Content.
          [*He proceeds towards the vault.*

THE BISHOP.
                                   Fall back,
There is yet time.

THE MONK (*marching toward the vault*).
          Introibo.

THE BISHOP.
          Reflect.

THE MONK (*with eyes raised to heaven*).
Smite thou, O God, thy prophet and thy priest,
And may thine awful will be done.
          [*He goes to the vault, and stops at the brink.*

THE BISHOP.
                              Thou owest
Obedience to thy bishop. He offends
His brethren, who amid the cloister's shades
Lifts up too bold a head. The Church is bound
To plunge in night the man who mars her peace.

THE MONK (*standing on the threshold of the vault*).
Amen!

THE BISHOP.
          Yield, monk, I summon thee to yield
Obedience.

######## THE MONK.
No.

######## THE BISHOP.
Descend a step.

[THE MONK *puts one foot within the vault, and goes down the first step.*

Recant; In Jesus' name I ask thee.

######## THE MONK.
No.

######## THE BISHOP.
Descend.

[THE MONK *goes down a second step.*

Abjure thy error.

######## THE MONK.
No.

######## THE BISHOP.
Descend.

[THE MONK *goes down a third step.*

I am Thy bishop and thy judge.   Retract thy false
And barbarous doctrine.

######## THE MONK.
No; for it is true.

######## THE BISHOP.
Submit to me.

######## THE MONK.
I cannot.

######## THE BISHOP.
Then, descend.

[THE MONK *goes down. Only half of his body is seen.* THE BISHOP *advances towards the opening. He shows* THE MONK *the interior.*

A cruse of water and a barley loaf
Thou seest there. Soon shall the curtain close
That shuts out day from thee. Soon shall the stars
And sunlight be hid from thee.

THE MONK.
Be it so.

THE BISHOP.
Descend.
[*He does so, only his head now appearing above the sepulchre.*
Bethink thee yet. Here, like a torch,
Without one breath of air, in hunger, thirst,
Thy life must pass away. Oh, such a death
Is horrible!

THE MONK.
It is sublime.

THE BISHOP.
Descend.
[THE MONK *disappears in the vault.*

THE MONK (*in the tomb*).
My feet have reached the floor.

THE BISHOP.
Place over him
That flagstone.

THE MONK.
Do so.
[*At a sign from* THE BISHOP, *two Monks roll the flagstone over the entrance to the vault. They do not, however, close it entirely, but leave a small vent-hole, over which* THE BISHOP *leans.*

THE BISHOP.

In the name of Christ!
And by Saint Peter's ring! wilt thou retract?
The night awaits thee when all hope is past.

THE MONK.

No.

THE BISHOP.

Thou hast but a moment more. Renounce
Thy wild and reckless errors.

THE MONK.

No.

THE BISHOP.

Then, go
In peace!
[*The two Monks push the flagstone, and the sepulchre is shut.*

And now, my brethren, let us pray.
[*They all join their hands together. The monks form in procession two by two, and march away slowly and solemnly, with* THE BISHOP *walking last. They disappear under the trees, chanting the prayer for the dead. Their voices gradually grow weaker.*

VOICES OF MONKS (*in the distance*).

De profundis ad te clamavi, Domine.

THE VOICE (*in the tomb*).

Have mercy, Lord, on this most wretched world!

VOICES OF MONKS.

Libera nos.

THE VOICE (*in the tomb*).

O God, deliver me!
[*Enter* DON SANCHO *and* DONNA ROSE.

SCENE VIII.

THE MONK *in the vault;* DON SANCHO, DONNA ROSE. DON SANCHO *and* DONNA ROSE *step out from the copse. They stop at the edge of the wood, and gaze at each other and at the solitude around them. A few moments' silence. It is almost night.*

DON SANCHO.

Because our love began in childhood's hour,
Our souls commingle, and my hand seeks thine;
And whether I draw thee, or thou dost me,
I cannot tell. There is some mystery, Rose,
That hovers over us, and sometimes haunts
My dreams. We have been reared together here
Within these walls. Who are we, dost thou know?
Why are we prisoners? But why should I care,
Since I to love thee am left free? Thou art
My lady, and I am thine own true knight.
I know not why I should speak of my soul.
My soul! it is the fragrant breath to which
Thy lips give issue; 't is the heavenly fire
That beams from out thine eyes. I have no soul
When thou 'rt no longer by. A kiss. — Thy veil
Annoys me.

DONNA ROSE.
   No.
[*She lets him kiss her, then leans on his arm and points to the sky.*

    See yonder star.
    [*Both gaze on the heavens with ecstasy.*

THE VOICE (*in the tomb*).
      O God!
Save, save the world!

VOICES OF MONKS (*in the distance*).
Ite, pax sepulcris!

THE VOICE (*in the tomb*).
Save, save!

DONNA ROSE.
Dost hear monks chanting?

DON SANCHO.
No. I hear
A cry.

VOICES OF MONKS (*growing fainter*).
Onus grave super caput.

DONNA ROSE.
It was the chanting of the monks; thou seest
How tender is the night when songs of praise
Rise through its dusky shades, an offering meet
For heaven! Throughout the earth there's naught but
love.
Then let us love each other!

VOICES OF MONKS.
Miserere!

THE VOICE (*in the tomb*).
Miserere!

DON SANCHO.
No, no. It is a cry.
Some one is calling. I was right. Whence comes
That cry?

DONNA ROSE.
'T is from the chapel. 'T is the hymn
Of evening.

DON SANCHO.
No.
DONNA ROSE.
The mists of night are apt
To mock our senses.

DON SANCHO (*noticing the stone that closes the vault*).
It is there!

DONNA ROSE.
I'm frightened.
DON SANCHO.
There is some one beneath!

DONNA ROSE.
The dead to speak!

THE VOICE (*in the tomb*).
O God! eternal Father!

DON SANCHO.
'Neath that stone
A living man is buried.

DONNA ROSE.
Go not near.
Some ghost, I say, with bloodless, hideous face,
Will surely rise!

DON SANCHO (*almost violently*).
Come help me.
[*He kneels down and tries to move the stone. She kneels beside him and also attempts to raise it. He turns to her, smiling.*
If he is
A malefactor, let him have through thee

His pardon.   [*He stoops down over the stone and shouts.*
          Is there some one suffering here?

                    THE VOICE (*in the tomb*).
Is anybody near?   Help!

                         DON SANCHO.
                         Wait a moment.
               [*Both attempt to move the flagstone*
In vain we try to turn aside this stone.
Where find a lever?
[*He sees an iron cross, on a tomb near the wall, a few steps
   from him.*
                         Ah, that cross!
                    [*Rising and going to the cross*

          DONNA ROSE (*stopping him*).
                              Take care!
     DON SANCHO (*looking at the tomb*).
Alas, poor man!

                    DONNA ROSE.
                    I dread to see you touch
That cross, a holy thing.

                    DON SANCHO.
                         It will be holier
When it has saved him.   If I pull it down
Christ will approve my deed.   [*He removes the cross.*

     DONNA ROSE (*making the sign of the cross*).
                         O crux, ave!

     DON SANCHO (*examining the cross, which he grasps with
                    both hands*).
A solid iron bar.   Now for a stone.

[*He rolls a block of stone near the tomb, and uses it as a fulcrum for his lever. He then introduces the point of the upper arm of the cross under the flagstone, and both endeavour to bend the bar.*

Ah! death likes not his eyelids to be opened.
'T is hard.
[*They stop a moment to recover breath.*
A convent is a curious place,
And sometimes is the scene of gloomy deeds.

DONNA ROSE.

O God! I shake with fear.

DON SANCHO (*leaning heavily on the lever*).
This flagstone is
Exceeding heavy.

DONNA ROSE.

It gives way! It swerves.
[*The stone begins to move.*

DON SANCHO.

One effort more. Give me a little help.
[ROSE *throws all her weight on the bar.* SANCHO *pushes the stone back. The vault is uncovered.*

DONNA ROSE (*clapping her hands*).

Well done!

DON SANCHO (*gazing into the dark vault*).
Ah, what a ghastly den! 'T is thick
With hideous fog.
[THE MONK *comes out slowly from the vault. He fixes his eyes by turns on* DON SANCHO *and* DONNA ROSE.

DONNA ROSE.

          A living man!   Why, yes!
It is the monk, the old man whom we saw!
What happiness is ours to have been there,
And to have heard him!

THE MONK.

                You have saved me, children
I swear the debt I owe I will repay.

ACT II.

THE THREE PRIESTS.

SCENE. — *In Italy. The top of a mountain. A hermit's grotto. At the back, the entrance, opening on the sky.*
On the ground in a corner, a straw mat. In the corner opposite, a little altar on which rests a death's head. In a hollow of the rock, a pitcher of water, a black loaf, a wooden dish on which are seen apples and chestnuts. A stone here and there for a seat, a larger one for a table. Forests on the horizon. Precipices, slopes parched by the sun and crossed by ravines. In the distance, a torrent. Through the mist, the belfry of a monastery.

SCENE I.

FRANCIS DE PAULA *alone. He is praying on his knees. He suddenly stops and rises. He listens. A confused noise of trumpets, horns, and barking is heard.*

FRANCIS.

What are those sounds I hear? It surely must
Be an illusion. 'T is the bell. [*He listens.*] No, 't is
A horn. A horn that sounds from rock to rock!
[*He listens.*] The torrent sometimes seems a host of voices
Rent by the wind and mingling with the breeze
That howls through forests. [*Listening.*] No; it is the
 chase. [*He looks outside.*
Oh! how the pack and whoop and trumpet blast
Do scare the mystic groves, and, to the ken
Of beast, man changes to a demon now.
[*He listens. The din of the hunt becomes more and more distinct.*
A fearful scandal this! Since Dorothy

And Simon first came here, the hermit shared
His cavern with the wolf alone, on this
Most hallowed waste, the Holy Father's fief,
Beneath the shelter of thick-spreading boughs;
They leagued together in fraternal love,
And man and nature were at peace. No one
The right doth hold, though he be prince or king,
To break the silence of these rugged woods
With hounds and horns and shouts, intruding on
A sacred mountain the tiara rules.
[*The barking is farther off. The clamour of the hunt is
now close by, now at a distance, ceases a moment, and
then begins again.*
The right to do so is the Pope's alone,—
A right he must not use, for he is but
A hunter after souls. No, even men
Stained with the vilest and most hideous crimes,
Would shrink from bloodshed in this holy place,
And from disturbing heaven's winged creatures, who
Are God's own care. And yet some one has dared
To do this wrong. Who can the caitiff be?
[*An aged monk, with staff in hand and feet covered with
dust, appears at the entrance to the grotto. He wears
a pilgrim's mantle over a Dominican habit. It is
TORQUEMADA. He stops at the threshold. His beard
is gray; that of FRANCIS DE PAULA white.*

SCENE II.

Francis de Paula, Torquemada.

TORQUEMADA.

Hail! venerable father!

FRANCIS.

Brother, hail!

TORQUEMADA.

May I rest here a moment?

FRANCIS.

Brother, enter.

TORQUEMADA.

I have toiled on, consumed by heat and cold,
And chilling fevers and the burning sun.
O holy patriarch! the man who seeks
The shelter of thy roof is all-unworthy!
Ah! I am very weary, and I say:
Lamma sabacthani! God bless thee, priest!

FRANCIS.

God bless thee, man.

TORQUEMADA.

I also am a priest.

FRANCIS.

'T is well. God be your guide. It is your right
To tell or not to tell from whence you come
And where you go; we all come from the dawn
And all go to the grave. And what you are,
My unknown brother, we are too. My son,
Infinitude weighs over all alike,

And mortals must all travel the same road.
We kneel before the altar, but our feet
Are at the tomb.

TORQUEMADA.

From out the Universe
I come, and to the City go. I go
To Rome.

FRANCIS.

To Rome?

TORQUEMADA.

Yes, I, so mean and vile,
Have yet a work to do, for which the time
Has come. I have, alone, and at a venture,
With naked feet, set out, and forced my way
Through snows and burning sands. My suit has reached
The Holy See. I know Pope Alexander
The Sixth.

FRANCIS.

What! our new Pope?

TORQUEMADA.

He is like me,
A Spaniard. At Valencia we have known
Each other well. His name is Borgia.
But who art thou, O reverend priest, whom God
Has guided to this lonely spot, content
To dwell in this rude cell? What is thy name?

FRANCIS.

Francis de Paula. You are?

TORQUEMADA.

Torquemada.
[*He draws back reverently before the hermit.*
Francis de Paula! Saint! Thou art a prophet!

FRANCIS.

No.

TORQUEMADA.

But thou dost work miracles, O father!
As it is said?

FRANCIS.

I see them, when the dawn
Doth every morning silver all the streams,
And when the giant sun comes forth to glad
The little birds, and when in field and grove
The all-embracing festival of Nature
Is set for hungry mouths, and all the dark
Bursts into life, and flowers unfold, and heaven
Through all its azure vastness shines; but 't is
Not I who work this miracle, 't is God.

TORQUEMADA.

O Father, Christ has brought us face to face!
Give ear unto the words of me, the seer,
Thou who art the apostle. Hast thou not
At times reflected on the thrice-crowned Pope,
That whited sepulchre, and hast thou not
Bethought thee that some obscure man might be
The loyal priest before the pontiff false,
And that while prostrate, as in duty bound,
Before the haughty vicar crowned by chance,
This pensive stranger bore within himself
That church's very soul whose diadem
The other vainly wears? What wouldst thou say
If such a chieftain of the faith, if such
An unknown victor, in thy presence stood?

FRANCIS.

The Pope, the man of God, bears sway. Two Romes
Do not exist.

TORQUEMADA.

No one is man of God
If he be not the man of men. Such man
Am I. Hell and its blackness lie in wait
For all the universe. I am the surgeon
With blood-bespattered hands. Unruffled, calm,
He saves, and yet seems horrible. So I,
The dread of all, through pity terrible,
But safe to realize my sacred aim,
Rush into that abyss whose name is Love.

FRANCIS.

I do not understand you. Let us pray.
[*He kneels before the altar.*

TORQUEMADA.

One day, erstwhile, when I was young, and wore
This robe but for a season, I beheld
A globe in Santa Cruz de Segovia
On which was traced the world with all its states,
Its rivers, forests, — all the earth, a heap
Of empires, countries, boundaries, and towns;
The snow-capped hills, and seas with islands strewn,
And all the depths in which the human race
Do fret and worry, swarming in the night.
Thou knowest, father, every emperor,
Be he or Christian or idolater,
A globe holds in his hand. This vision I
Have had before mine eyes: the universe,
With all its zones and nations, — Africa
And Europe; India, where the dawn is born;
And I have said, The point in question is
How to become the master of it all;
And I have said, The point in question is
To rule all this for Jesus, who in dreams

Hath often called on me for help. We must
Take hold of earth and give it back to heaven.
Yes, father, yes, this earthly sphere, with all
Its cries and wars, its kingdoms and its din,
Is mine, — dost hear? — is mine!

FRANCIS (*rising and laying a finger on the death's head*).
                              Behold my sphere!
This relic of the fate that wrecks and fails,
The contemplation of this dark enigma,
The shadow that eternity casts o'er
This thought-awakening nothingness, this skull
That, like a reef, shoots from the human gulf,
Those teeth that hold the smile with which they gleamed
At their first dawning, though the eyes have lost
Their whilom light, this hideous mask we all
Wear 'neath our brows, this spectre that discerns
That which is veiled from us, this fragment, taught
The mysteries of the unknown bourn — ah! yes,
To see below that frigid gaze my soul,
My naked soul, and, thinking, musing thus,
Grow old and feel that life is less and less,
With these two dark, fixed holes for witnesses,
To pray and meditate upon this dust,
This nullity, this silence in the shade
That listens to my prayers. Lo! all I have;
It is enough for me.

TORQUEMADA (*aside*).
                    A lightning flash
Darts through my soul while listening to his words.
Once Constantine — well worthy ruling he —
Saw hover in the air the labarum.
                     [*Pointing to the death's head.*
And I, like Constantine, behold that sign,

And I like him shall conquer by it. Yes,
This holy hermit shows my dazzled eyes
The other form of faith, the other light
By which the Christian's guided. Yes, I shall
Hold fast my sphere, and from him shall take his,
So that the shoal may mark where is the port,
And death become life's banner!
    [*To* FRANCIS DE PAULA.] Pray, give ear.
Saint Dominick has wrongly understood
The sense of fire, which is sublime, unless
It be most infamous. To punish was
His aim; mine is to save, to light anew
The stakes that have been quenched. My meaning is
Apparent to thee now?

FRANCIS.

It is.

TORQUEMADA.

I wish
To light on earth the countless, saving flames.
O father, none before me has e'er dreamed
Of better gift to man; and in my sleep
My Jesus comes and says: "Go one Go on!
If thou dost reach the goal thou aimest at,
That shall be warrant for thy deeds!" I go!
[FRANCIS DE PAULA *places on the big stone that serves as*
a table the loaf, the plate of chestnuts, and the pitcher
of water.

FRANCIS.

There thou hast water, bread, and chestnuts. Drink
To quench thy thirst, and eat to still thy hunger.
As to thy plans, whose end I dimly see,
I pray that for thy sake God's thunderbolts
May strike thee dead, before a single stake
Shall flame to heaven; 't wou'l be better far

For thee, my son, and for the human race
That thou shouldst die, ere thou hadst power to take
One step in such a path!

TORQUEMADA (*aside*).

How feeble grows
The mind that lives alone! For this poor saint
My purpose has no meaning.

FRANCIS.

Man was placed
On earth to love all things, the brother, friend
Of every creature. If he kill a worm,
He must know why. God of the human soul
Has made a sheltering wing that spreads itself
O'er all creation. Man cannot decree
The doom of anything that lives on earth,
In air, or sea, or under verdant boughs.
To men the liberty to toil; to birds
The freedom of the grove; to all be peace,
But neither chain nor cage. If man becomes
An executioner, God is a tyrant.
The Gospel has the cross, the sword, the Koran.
Let us transform all sorrow and all wrong
Into a blessing on this dismal earth.
Who smites may err; then let us never smite.
Ah! son, the scaffold is a dreadful challenge.
Leave death to God. What! Make the tomb your agent?
What arrogance! The child, the dove, the woman,
The flower, the fruit, all's sacred, all is blessed;
And when by night or day I meditate,
And from this lofty pinnacle pour out
An all-embracing prayer into the depths,
Within me stirs the boundless power of love.
As for the Pope, my son, he is the Pope,

And we must reverence him. The great law is
To always pardon and to always hope,
Never to doom to death a living creature,
And if we see another's fault, to make
Atonement for that fault ourselves, to pray,
Believe, adore, — such is the law, my son,
And it is mine. Who keeps that law is saved.

TORQUEMADA.

Thou savest but thyself, old man! But how
About the others? Ah! the eternal loss
Of souls, my father! Every moment sees
The fatal plunge into the flames of hell,
Into the horrors of the yawning gulf!
All night and day the black abyss lies open.
Ah! yes, thou sav'st thyself! What dost thou, though
To save thy brother man? In calm content
Thou livest on thy apples and thy nuts,
Another Anselm or Pacomus in
The Lybian desert, and thou art no more
The world's debtor, and all things go well,
And nothing horrible lurks round! For hell,
And darkness, and the doom of souls accursed, —
What carest thou? Thou hast thy bed of straw
And cruse of water, and canst meditate,
Alone! — alone! A child might live such life,
But not a man. There dwells, then, not in thee
The awful, holy fatherhood of God!
The human family which he created,
Is it of no account? Why, we regard
The welfare of an ox, we cure a dog!
And man's in peril! Thou art pitiless!
Thou livest here beneath the vault of heaven,
Far from the haunts of man, and dost not feel
That by a thousand ties thou still art bound
To man, — to noxious, dreadful, impious man!

Who in the cavern's depths or on the heights
Still drags with him through every place his woes
From which distil his crimes! These spreading ills
Come not near thee! What, then! the living pass
Before thine eyes, and yet thou feelest not
Thy shadow links thee to those phantoms dark!
Ah, yes! indeed, thy hands are meekly crossed!
And thou dost chant the Psalms, and go and come
From cross to altar, from yon pile of stone
To this small piece of wood! 'T is isolation!
When everything is tottering, crumbling, sinking,
Old man, thy duty is amid the throng!
Yes, duty, rigorous, implacable,
Whose biting sting is felt within the conscience,
Doth tear thee from the cloister's solitude,
And cry: "Help, help! think of the human race!
Think of the multitude! Awake from sleep!
On, on!" — O God! must little children burn
In endless pangs! Must women, aged men,
Nay, all mankind sink in this howling Sodom!
Haste! save these souls accursed, against their will,
And force them to return to Paradise!
Old man, it is for this we are on earth.
Thy law is light; my law is mystery.
Thou art but hope, and I salvation am.
I am God's helper.

[*For some time a man has been standing on the threshold of the entrance. He is also old and gray-bearded. He has a hunting-spear in his hand and a three-branched cross on his breast He is dressed in a hunting suit of gold brocade, and wears a cap of gold with three circles of pearls. He has a horn at his belt. He has heard the last words of* FRANCIS DE PAULA, *and listened to those of* TORQUEMADA *He bursts out laughing* FRANCIS DE PAULA *and* TORQUEMADA *turn round.*

SCENE III.

The same. THE HUNTER.

THE HUNTER.

Well! upon my faith,
My lute-players could not amuse me more
Than you have done, my children. I have been
A well-pleased listener. You 're a pair of fools.
I left my dogs and nets and springes yonder,
And said: I will climb up and have a look
At this old fellow. So you see me here.
You have diverted me. But, on the whole,
Life would be very tiresome if it were
What you have called it.
 [*He advances, folds his arms, and looks them in the face*
                        God — if he exist,
He 's silent — made a silly masterpiece
When he made man. But in the gradual growth
From worm to snake, from snake to dragon, and
From dragon to the devil, there is grandeur.
                        [*He takes a step toward* TORQUEMADA
I know thee, Torquemada. Get thee gone.
Return into thy country. I received
Thy suit. 'T is granted. Go, my son. Thine is
A grand idea. It has made me laugh.
Go back to Spain, and do all that thou wilt.
The goods the Jews possess I grant my nephew.
My son, you asked why man is on the earth,
And I shall give the reason in two words.
What need to hide the truth? Life is enjoyment.
My friends, I can see naught beyond this world,
And in this world I see myself. For each

A word shines through the different prisms. For thee,
The meaning of that word is prayer, for me
'T is pleasure.

TORQUEMADA (*gazing alternately at* FRANCIS DE PAULA
and THE HUNTER).
Both are egotists alike.

THE HUNTER.
Chance and the fitting moment worked the clay,
And the amalgam's man. Now, as, like you,
I am but matter merely, should I not
A senseless dullard be to hesitate
And play the sluggard when joy speeds so fast,
Nor have delight of all, when all is fleeting?
The chief concern of man is to be happy.
Whatever men call crime or vice I take
Into my service. Murder? an expedient.
Incest? a prejudice. I honour conscience
By bidding her a courteous good-bye.
Do you believe that, if my daughter's fair,
I would be shy in seeking for her love?
Bah! I am not an idiot. I must live.
Go ask the falcon, eagle, and the hawk
If they know from what nest their prey has come.
Because you wear a habit black or white,
You think you're forced to be absurd and timid,
And lower your eyes before the boundless bliss
The giddy universe spreads out before you.
Let us be wise and profit by the time.
Beyond death there is naught, let us live well!
The ball-room crumbles and becomes a tomb.
The sage's soul trips dancing to the grave.
Serve up my banquet. If to-day there's need
To season some one else's feast with poison,

Let it be done. Why should the death of others
Disturb me? I have life. I am a vast
Insatiate, rabid hunger, and the world
Is in my eyes the fruit to be devoured.
O death, I will forget that thou art real.
I do not know thee, God. While I'm alive,
I make haste to be happy; when I'm dead,
I simply disappear.

     FRANCIS (*to* TORQUEMADA).
      I pray you say
Who is this bandit?
     TORQUEMADA.
      Father, 't is the Pope.

TORQUEMADA

PART II.

DRAMATIS PERSONÆ.

TORQUEMADA.
DON SANCHO.
DONNA ROSE.
THE MARQUIS DE FUENTEL.
KING FERDINAND.
QUEEN ISABELLA.
GUCHO.
THE BISHOP OF URGEL.
THE KING'S CHAPLAIN.
MOSES BEN HABIB, *Grand Rabbi.*
THE DUKE D'ALAVA.
AN USHER.

Soldiers, Pages, Monks, Jews. Black and white penitents

ACT I.

SCENE. — *The royal patio, called "Condes-reyes," in the convent-palace of Llana at Burgos. A square court surrounded by a gallery with trilobate arcades. One of the sides of this gallery in front of the theatre. The court has two great public gates, facing each other and opening on the city beyond. The gallery in the foreground abuts, on the left, on a folding-door, closed and raised above a flight of three steps. On the right, it communicates with an outer porch which is a kind of lodge. Near this outer porch, on a dais, is a high iron chair, blazoned and crowned with a pinnacle, above which is placed a sword, the point unsupported. In the outer porch are seen two priests, motionless, who seem charged with the care of a chest placed on the floor.*

SCENE I.

DON SANCHO, THE MARQUIS DE FUENTEL, *then* GUCHO. DON SANCHO *is dressed in cloth of gold. He has a sword at his side.*

DON SANCHO.
But surely 't is a dream!

THE MARQUIS.
No, it is real.

DON SANCHO.
I am a prince!

THE MARQUIS.
Count King of Burgos.

DON SANCHO.
I!

THE MARQUIS.

Except our sovereign lord, Don Ferdinand,
You hold the highest rank throughout this province.
      [*He kisses the hand of* DON SANCHO
The world is yours, for you have happiness
And greatness.

DON SANCHO.
    Yes! for Rose will be my bride!

THE MARQUIS.
Within an hour. They're putting on her crown.
The chapel's almost fitted up, and prayers
Have been begun. The Bishop of Urgel
Will celebrate the marriage. I arrange
The ceremony. So the King has ordered.

DON SANCHO.
You, our good genius!

THE MARQUIS.
     Donna Rose awaits
Your presence in this cloister, while the altar
Is being lighted. I, Gil de Fuentel,
Will open for you yonder door, so that
Your Highness may, as custom bids, seek out
Your future bride, and lead her here to pay
The homage which is due your suzerain,
And thank him for his grace. Before your marriage
The King would speak to you. Such is his wish.
He will be in that gallery.

DON SANCHO.
     I would
Prefer to go to church.

THE MARQUIS.
                    You must obey.
The King, my lord, will simply say these words:
"I give consent." Besides, it is a custom
Come down from elder time, because your crown
Of his is vassal.
            DON SANCHO.
    Be it so.

            THE MARQUIS.
                    You must
Conform to legal usage.
            DON SANCHO.
                So, my father —

            THE MARQUIS.
Was Jorge, the Infante of Burgos.

            DON SANCHO.
His father was —
        THE MARQUIS (*aside*).
    Myself!

            DON SANCHO.
                    The King, from whom
The Infante sprung.
            THE MARQUIS.
                A long and prosperous reign
Awaits your Highness. Let my counsels shape
Your course.
            DON SANCHO.
        I yield blindfolded to your guidance.
I know not why it is: I think you love me.
And still, it is not long since first we met.
One day you brought an order — how we feared you! —
To Rose and me to leave that convent old.

And come in presence of our lord. When we
Reached here, I was afraid. It almost looked
As if we were some captured prey. But now
We are allowed to marry, and with joy
My heart is filled. And, when by you, I feel
My happiness secure.

THE MARQUIS.

Depend on me.
That happiness is my sole care, and I
To God entrust your sacred head. If you
Lay dying on a bed of torturing pain,
And if, as happened to the Count de Retz,
You needed for your safety draughts of blood,
What bliss were mine to open all my veins,
That while I died you might be born again
Of mine own life, — my prince, my king, my lord!
[*Aside.*] My child!
[*Enter* GUCHO. *He hears the last words of* THE MARQUIS.

GUCHO (*aside, observing* THE MARQUIS).

How kind he looks! — triumphant too
Some mystery here! But bah! why should I care?
I 'm placed too far beyond the sphere of man
E'en to be curious about such things.
And though by motion of this little finger
I might prevent all ill, achieve all good,
I would not wag it. No, my business is
To be a creeping thing, a looker-on, —
And to be valueless.
[*Enter a company of soldiers of the African guard of the
King of Castile, having at their head* THE DUKE OF
ALAVA, *their captain.*

THE MARQUIS (*to* DON SANCHO).

The King, my lord,
Will in a moment 'neath that peristyle

Receive your Highness.
[*He mounts the steps of the perron, and throws back the leaves of the folding-door opening on the interior of the convent-palace. He makes a sign to* Don Sancho *to follow him*

       Enter, prince.
[*He sees the soldiers, and points them out to* Don Sancho.
          This guard
Is there to do you honour.
[*He continues his discourse with* Don Sancho *while the latter is mounting the steps.*
       When you hear
The trumpets sound, your Highness shall conduct
The Countess to the King, and both shall kneel.
      [*He casts a look beyond the gallery.*
Ah, 't is the King.
[Don Sancho *enters through the folding-door, and after him* The Marquis de Fuentel. *The door closes on them. Enter* The King, *followed by his chaplain.*

SCENE II.

The King, Gucho, The Duke of Alava, *a chaplain of the King.*

    the king (*to* The Duke).
  Here, Duke.
    [The Duke *approaches* The King.]
       When from my neck
I take this collar off, and on his neck
I place it —
    the duke.
  Sire, I hear.

THE KING (*looking on the company of guards*).
                    They're there.   'T is well.
[*To* THE DUKE.]   When you shall hear me say: "I dub thee knight,
Now thou art King.   God have thee in his keeping!"
Then, Duke, behind him you shall draw your sword,
And you shall kill him.

THE DUKE.
                    Sire, it is enough.

GUCHO (*aside, pressing his two bawbles to his heart*).
My dolls are in more safety than are men.
[THE CHAPLAIN *leans towards the ear of* THE KING, *and points to the chest guarded by the two Priests standing under the outer porch.*

CHAPLAIN (*in a low voice to* THE KING).
The robes of serge are here, and all prepared,
According to your Majesty's command.

THE KING.
I do not think they will be needed; still
                    [*Pointing to the outer porch.*
Remain beneath the vault.
[THE CHAPLAIN *joins the two Priests under the outer porch.*
THE KING *turns to the Captain of the guards.*
                    You, Duke, stay there.
[*Aside.*]   In either case I will have nigh at hand
The means of compassing the issue which
I deem most suitable.
[*The folding-door opens, giving entrance to* THE MARQUIS DE FUENTEL, *and then closes again.* THE KING *has remarked the iron chair, and has begun to gaze earnestly at it.*

SCENE III.

The same, THE MARQUIS.

THE MARQUIS (*aside*).
     Within an hour
He shall be married, — my young prince and count.
Each moment that glides past is but a round
By which he mounts from out the depths of night
Towards the radiant dawn. Another step
And he is happy, powerful, august!
Oh, what a gleam of light this sinless child
Has shed upon a grandsire's infamy!
And I can weep to think this shrunken soul,
So vile and dark, has still within itself
A something that expands, O merciful God,
Beneath thy gracious power! [*He dries his eyes.*

THE KING (*turning round*).
     Ah, you are here!

THE MARQUIS (*bowing*).
My liege —

THE KING.
   I shall be highly pleased to hold
Some converse with you, Marquis.
    [*He points to the old iron chair.*
     What's this chair?
And why the sword above it?

THE MARQUIS.
    Please your grace,
That is the throne on which Don Garcia sat,
Your ancestor. The sword is placed above,
To symbolize a kingly attribute.

THE KING.

'T is right.   In this my realm I am the source
Of life and death.

GUCHO (*to* THE KING).
But there are two of you!

[*For some moments a procession has been debouching through
the door on the right into the square court, and moving
towards the door on the left. It consists of two files of
penitents, — one black, the other white. They march
parallel to each other, with slow steps, their cowls hiding their faces. The cowls of the black penitents are
white, those of the white penitents black. The cowls
have holes for the eyes. At the head of the two files,
a black penitent with black cowl bears a black banner,
on which is seen a death's head above two bones in the
form of a cross. The death's head is white as well as
the two cross bones. The procession moves across the
back of the theatre with slow steps and in silence.*
GUCHO *points out the banner to* THE KING.

THE KING (*to* GUCHO).

You speak the truth!   That abject monk!

GUCHO.
Agreed.
He 's abject, but he 's great.   When Torquemada
Presents himself, all tremble, even you.

THE MARQUIS.

That banner seems to bring with it the smell
Of smoking flesh, the odour of the stake.

THE KING.

Where go they, Marquis?

GUCHO.
                    In pursuit of those
Who shall be burned on the public square.
You are, mayhap, a simple citizen.
Straightway, without an inkling of the reason,
You find yourself enmeshed in some dark plot;
Or you have said one day a silly word
By your fireside, without a thought of harm;
Scarce has that fatal word escaped your lips,
When it takes flight towards the Holy Office,
And sinks into that dismal ear which lies
Uncovered in the night. Then issues forth
From out a cloister crowned by gloomy domes
Yon banner heading its two rows of phantoms,
And the procession slowly marches on.
No obstacle arrests its course. It moves
Across or through the things and men it meets,
And when it shows itself all take to flight,
Or fall upon the earth, for they behold
The dread familiars of the Inquisition:
They know that vision is a hand that goes
To clutch some victim sitting by his hearth.
So, in this guise, it moves through all the city,
[*Pointing to the banner and the two files of cowled men
    passing at the back of the court of honour.*
Just as you see it now — by day or night.
It goes straight to its aim, mute, terrible,
Without or cry or chant. You're in your house,
Perhaps you have sat down at table, or,
With laugh and innocent chatter, pluck the flowers
Your garden bears or kiss your children, when
That death's head comes upon you in the shade.
What numbers have been burned, — a countless host!
Whoever sees that standard march towards him
Is hopeless and undone.

[*The procession and banner disappear through the great door of the court opposite that by which they have entered.*]

    THE MARQUIS (*in a low voice to* THE KING).
        The clergy are
Too highly favoured by their prince. What then!
This Torquemada dares to hold at Rome
A secret council, parleys with the Pope,
Brings back a bull, and lo! this is enough
To throw the King into the shade! And so
His power resplendent, gladdening every eye,
Sinks into blackness! Sire, this monk usurps.
He has in some few years his sordid head
Placed on a level with the crowns of kings.
[THE KING *seems distracted, and not to pay any attention to the words of* THE MARQUIS, *who says in a low voice to* GUCHO:
He does not listen.

    GUCHO (*in a low tone to* THE MARQUIS).
       'T is because his mind
Is taken up with something else.
[THE KING *raises his head. At a sign from him all the persons present fall back. He beckons to* THE MARQUIS *to approach. He leads him to the front of the stage, so that no one can hear what he is about to say.* GUCHO *is watching them.*

    THE KING (*to* THE MARQUIS).
         I have
On all occasions followed your advice,
And it has been my gain, for there are none
Whose council, Marquis, I prefer to yours.

I wish, then, to consult you on a matter
That must be settled quickly, even here.
[THE KING *perceives* GUCHO, *who has remained behind the
  dais of the iron throne. At a gesture from* THE KING,
  GUCHO *goes off.*

GUCHO (*aside, looking at* THE KING *and* THE MARQUIS).
Young tiger and old cat! What's happening now?

SCENE IV.

THE KING, THE MARQUIS *in front of the stage. The
  other bystanders at the back, beyond reach of their
  voices.*

THE KING.
I know how prudent all your counsel is,
And it shall be my guide.

THE MARQUIS (*aside*).
                    And I know too
What all this signifies. Your Highness will
Precisely do the very opposite
Of what I may advise.

THE KING.
                    Are you content
With matters as they stand in Europe now?
Do you, so subtle an intriguer, see
Aught that is likely to hold stable there?

THE MARQUIS.
A dike. That dike is you. Alone you stand
Erect. All else goes down before the power

Of ever-growing France.   Yet, sire, you are
On one point vulnerable, on Navarre;
For there your frontier's open.   But you have,
Of your own wondrous wisdom, seen the ill
And found the cure long ere we thought of it,
And taken Sancho from the cardinal,
That poor old kinglet of Orthez, and now
The scale leans to your Highness' side at last.
You have the power, Don Sancho has the right.
The colossus you are, the lever he.
You hold him, like an eagle that has seized
An eaglet in his talons.   He alone
Of all on earth is needful to your power.
While he's alive, France will be held in check.

THE KING.
He needful to me! — he, and he alone!

THE MARQUIS.
With Donna Rose.

THE KING.
     So then you think I ought
To let Don Sancho live?

THE MARQUIS.
    Most surely, yes.

THE KING.
Well, in a moment, when yon door is opened,
You'll see Don Sancho slain.
[*Movement of astonishment and terror by* THE MARQUIS.
      Rose pleases me.
Never did mirth and modesty combine
In loftier soul, and never maid did wed

Such charming voice to such a flashing eye;
She has so cruel and so sweet an air;
Her little feet this hand of mine could hold;
She trembles at a word, and thereby gives
A heightened loveliness to all her charms.
Now since she has enraptured me, the King,
Don Sancho's one too many.

THE MARQUIS.
                    Sire, you're right.
THE KING.
Ah! well I know state reasons bid the King
Withstand his lusts. What course then should I take?
This has not been a sudden whim of mine.
One wavers while a fire is waxing strong.
Think you I have not struggled?   I have said
To my own self, for in myself this strife
Had to be waged with tiresome stubbornness:
"The devil! she is pretty! — yes, but still
To me this marriage would be a great gain.
I need Navarre. Without Navarre I have
No frontier." — Love, keep quiet, I beseech! —
But then her eyes! her velvet skin! her grace!
"Hold, King! Wilt for a passing petticoat
Lose in one day the fruit of ten years' battles?
Direct thy gaze beyond the mountains there,
And see thyself the King of France's mock.
Suppose we marry Rose and Sancho, then,
The Durance and the Adour both are ours,
Our frontiers are arranged; so let us act
As every skilled, exalted statesman should.
Let them be wedded!" — No! what yoke is **mine**!
To see her pass into another's arms! —
No, never that! Perish my rival rather!
She is my prey. Am I a slave, and are

My sceptres tyrants? Must I mutilate
This heart of mine, and tear out every fibre,
Because a rabble rout of royal spies,
Who dwell upon the Seine, the Tiber, Rhine,
Are watching for the hour distraught ambition
Is off its guard? It is a grievous thing
To be a mighty king. The heart requires
Some compensation. I lament the fate
That forces me to have Don Sancho killed,
And killed here in his home, among his people;
But we 're not on this earth to bore ourselves.
Am I in fault because this girl is fair?

THE MARQUIS.

'T is really not your fault.

THE KING.

     I 'm tired to death
Of Isabel. I need another woman.
In short, I surely have the right to love.

THE MARQUIS.

The lion has the right to hunt for prey
When he is hungry.

THE KING.

    List! I love and hate.
I seem to see their childhood spent together,
That cloister's privacy, the grass and furze,
His daring and her grace, the shaded groves,
The kisses which this saucy fellow took!
This Sancho!— Ah! I 'm jealous, and would fain
Be rid of him! I like to count the throbs
Of sombre hatred in my wrathful heart,
And in my very hair would wish to feel
The fiery pulsings. It is good to hate,

To hold your enemy until you crush
And trample on him; ah! what savage joy!
I am the abyss rejoicing to engulf
This halcyon. I feel a tremulous force
Within me for destruction. Woe to him
Would try to change my course! No check avails.
I hold Don Sancho, and will have revenge!
Revenge for what?   Revenge because he's loved,
Because he's fair. I, who am dark and close,
Have in my soul a hundred storms that rush
From adverse quarters. Murder is my friend,
And Cains my brethren are, and while I look
With grave and glacial and half-sleeping eyes,
I feel the fell desires that fill my soul,
As the volcano, cold beneath its snows,
Feels that its lava mounts towards its mouth
In waves of blackness. He that would attempt
To calm my soul would make me rage the more.
Attempt to still me, and you drive me mad.
Yes, Marquis, I would shatter God himself! —
Two means exist by which I can get rid
Of the Infante.
    THE MARQUIS (*aside*).
  Two!

     THE KING.
      One sad, the cloister;
The other quick and sharp, the grave. Oh, yes,
The cloister's well. The tomb is better still.
It hears no sound within its safe abyss.
The cloister may be dumb. The tomb is deaf,
And has this precious feature: none can leave it.
The cloister is an abject circle traced
By a grim compass. In it those who live
Turn round forever. In this fashion Sancho

Would see his fair locks change to white, and, pale,
Would grow to age, the gloomy temple's captive.
I have the choice. — I much prefer his death —
What do you think?

THE MARQUIS.
You're right.

THE KING.
Eh!

THE MARQUIS.
Let him die

THE KING (*aside*).
Why, who has whispered to me that he was
The father of Don Sancho? 'T is not true!

THE MARQUIS.
I think as you do.

THE KING (*aside*).
Oh, the lies that reach
The ears of kings!

THE MARQUIS (*watching him*).
Your purpose proves your wisdom.

THE KING.
Then you advise his death.

THE MARQUIS.
Yes, sire, I do.

THE KING (*aside*).
This is suspicious. He affirmed just now
That I had need of Sancho, and his life
Was bound up with the welfare of my state.
With Sancho dead, I have no longer claim

Upon Navarre. The Empire blocks the way
In one direction, and France in the other.
                      [*Watching* THE MARQUIS *closely.*
Where does this traitor wish to urge me on?
He has some scheme in hand. [*Aloud.*] It would be nice
To eat up Sancho all at once, but then
What if I nibbled at him? While he is
Within the cloister, he is near my teeth.
Suppose I kept him there to see him pine
And peak and grow more stupid every day?
A slow revenge gives a voluptuous joy.
What thinkest thou?

              THE MARQUIS.

                     Why choose a tortuous path?
No, sire, go straight towards the goal. Strike, kill!

              THE KING (*aside*).

The knave! Till now his every word was all
In favour of Don Sancho — He forgets,
      [*Watching* THE MARQUIS, *who is watching him.*
But I remember   Ah, the two-faced rogue!
But on his face I see a sudden gleam!
Why does he press me where my hatred leads?
How devilish quick he changed his views for mine!
[*Aloud to* THE MARQUIS.] But blood —

              THE MARQUIS.

                    The bloody kings have always had
The most devoted servants. Kill!

              THE KING (*aside*).

                          He is
A secret hireling of the King of France.
The scoundrel!

[*Aloud.*] But you lately used these words
'Don Sancho is your hope. You need his aid.
Peace is assured along the Pyrenees
While he is living."

THE MARQUIS.

Sire, I was deceived.
You're great, and have no need of any man;
No, not of God even. Kill!

THE KING.

You are sincere.
I feel it; but reflect. That set of beggars,
The people, take offence at those expedients
Which policy dictates. The mob is stirred
To pity from slight cause It takes to heart
A gash or two in some one's breast, and if
He is a handsome lad, it cries aloud.
Put me in prison, I am soon forgot,
But men weep round my bier. We should mistrust
The use of too harsh methods, my good friend.
Don Sancho's young, and tragedies suit not
The public taste; while many worthy folk
Would thank me for my clemency, if I
Should wall him in a convent. Clemency!
So beautiful a virtue! Let his home
Be in a cloister. Can he fly? Oh, no!

THE MARQUIS.

The grave would guard him closer.

THE KING.

But a murder—

THE MARQUIS (*pointing to the palace*).

'T is no unwonted guest within these walls.

THE KING (*aside*).

Ha, traitor!
[*Aloud.*] Then, what is your final word,
Good Marquis?

THE MARQUIS.

Kill! [*Flourish of trumpets.*
The trumpets! Here they come!
[*The folding-doors of the convent-palace open.* DON SAN-
CHO *and* DONNA ROSE *appear on the perron holding
each other's hand.* DONNA ROSE *in a robe of silver lace
with a crown of pearls on her head.* DON SANCHO
*with the cap of a count adorned with an aigrette com-
posed of plumes and precious stones. On the right of
the couple is* THE BISHOP OF URGEL, *a mitre on his
head. Behind them, ladies, lords, priests in embroidered copes.*

SCENE V.

The same. DON SANCHO, DONNA ROSE, THE BISHOP
OF URGEL.

THE BISHOP.

King Ferdinand, this man, Don Sancho, weds
This maiden, Donna Rose, and both are sprung
From Gothic kings, — she, Lady of Orthez;
He, Count of Burgos. Sire, if 't is your will
That I should marry them, I shall proceed.
Don Sancho with his bride, led by the priest,
Will kneel before you, sire, and pledge his faith,
For he is count and you are his liege lord
[DON SANCHO *and* DONNA ROSE *descend, advance towards*

THE KING *and kneel.* THE DUKE OF ALAVA *takes a step forward.* THE MARQUIS *watches him breathless.*

DON SANCHO.

My lordships, sire, I lay down at your feet.

THE KING (*looking earnestly at* THE BISHOP).

What is this madness, bishop? dost thou wed
A monk and nun?

THE BISHOP.

My liege! —

THE KING.

Art thou aware
That they have taken vows? And dost thou dare
To consummate this horrid sacrilege?

THE BISHOP.

Your Grace! —

THE KING.

A frock for him! a veil for her!
[*The chaplain and the priests issue from the outer porch. One of the priests holds a black veil in his hands, the other a robe of serge. The latter throws the frock over* DON SANCHO; *the former the veil over* DONNA ROSE. *The face of* DON SANCHO *disappears under the cowl, that of* DONNA ROSE *under the veil. The soldiers surround them. One of them snatches his sword from* DON SANCHO. THE KING *makes a furious gesture.*
Away with both! Each to a convent!

DON SANCHO (*struggling under the cowl*).

King!

THE KING (*to the priests*).

You'll answer to me for that man.

THE MARQUIS (*breathing again*).
                                    Alive!
[*The priests and soldiers lead off* DON SANCHO *and* DONNA ROSE *in different directions.*

THE KING (*to* THE MARQUIS *in a low voice*).
I'll have her back.   For sometimes, after all,
A woman leaves a cloister.

THE MARQUIS (*aside*).
                                    And a man!

ACT II.

SCENE.— *A hall of the old Moorish palace in Seville. This palace looks on the Tablada on which the Quemadero was placed. It is the Hall of the Council (del Consejo). At the back a gallery with Moorish columns opening on the exterior and closed by a vast curtain. On the left a long table, at the two extremities of which are placed two high arm-chairs surmounted by royal crowns. They are of the same height, and face each other. On the same side, in the tapestry, a secret door, low and narrow, communicating with a private staircase. On the opposite side, on the right, in a corner of the wall meeting the gallery at the back, large folding-doors above a flight of three steps. The table is covered with tapestry, embroidered with the arms of Castile and Aragon. In the middle of the table, on a large silver dish, are placed in rows thirty piles of gold crowns, high and thick, forming a square in the centre of the dish. On the table a silver-gilt inkstand, parchment, vellum, wax, seals. Gilt and coloured pens in the orifices of the inkstand. Near the table a sideboard with drawers.*

SCENE I.

THE MARQUIS DE FUENTEL, MOSES-BEN-HABIB, *Grand Rabbi. Both enter through the secret door.*

THE MARQUIS.

There's need of gold. Be lavish of your gold.
[THE GRAND RABBI *points to the dish loaded with crowns in the middle of the table.* THE MARQUIS *examines the heap of gold.*
Good.

THE RABBI.

Thirty piles of gold, and every pile
Contains a thousand crowns.

THE MARQUIS.
A first-rate plan.

THE RABBI.
The Queen is greedy.

THE MARQUIS.
And the King is thriftless.
Truth lodges at the bottom of a well;
Intrigue in golden mines. By dint of presents
The leave to live may be won from the great.
To 'scape a master or a cozening judge,
Or prince or priest, a poor man must be rich.
All kings are beggars, and require that alms
Be given without stint.
[*To* THE RABBI.] Away! Descend
The little staircase, Jew. The King is near.

THE RABBI.
Your goodness I implore, my lord. There still
Is time to save the Jewish people?

THE MARQUIS.
Yes.
The peril's urgent. [*Dismissing him.*] Go!

THE RABBI.
I count on you.

THE MARQUIS.
Nay, count upon thy gold.

THE RABBI.
Shall we be let,
A hopeless, weeping crowd, prostrate ourselves
Before the King and Queen?

THE MARQUIS.
                        Yes; be it so.
But, for the moment, go.

THE RABBI.
                  Oh, day of wrath!
A hundred aged Jews, unless the King
Be our protector, must be burned alive
Here, even in this city of Seville;
And all the rest, alas! must exiles be.

THE MARQUIS (*sad and thoughtful*).
Yes; all's prepared for that auto-da-fe
That has been long proclaimed.

THE RABBI.
                        Pray, is it true
The King this evening leaves?

THE MARQUIS.
                        Yes, for one day;
To-morrow he returns. Our oldest law
The charter of King Tulgas, sets apart
The morrow of an execution as
A day the King and Queen must spend in prayer
Within the convent of Triana.

THE RABBI.
                  Ah!
No need to offer prayers to save the dead,
If they who pray were not their slayers. Try
To save us, lord.

THE MARQUIS.
      Speak low, and get thee gone.
[THE GRAND RABBI *bows to the ground, and leaves through
    the door in the tapestry, which closes on him.*

THE MARQUIS (*gazing on the door by which he has left, aside*).
'T is not thy Jewish hide or people's woe
That stimulates my anguish and my zeal,
And drives me to risk all.   Alas! whene'er
I hear the hideous funeral knell that 's tolled
For the auto-da-fe, I shrink with dread.
Don Sancho 's in a convent, and declines
To be a monk, is stubborn and unyielding.
He may be flung at any moment on
The flaming stake.   I tremble for him.   Ah,
Thou frightful cloister, he must leave thee!   How?
[*The great door at the back opens.   Enter* THE KING. GUCHO *follows him.   The two leaves fall back.*   THE KING *in the full costume of Alcantara, with the sinople cross embroidered in emeralds on the mantle.   He has a cap of green velvet, without plume, encircled with a royal crown.* GUCHO *squats behind one of the armchairs.*

SCENE II.

THE MARQUIS, THE KING, GUCHO.   THE KING *seems to see nothing.   He appears to be deeply preoccupied.*

THE KING (*aside*).
No need to hurry matters.   Better wait.

THE MARQUIS (*to* THE KING, *making a reverence*).
A great disaster will occur to-day,
Unless the King prevent.
[THE KING *raises his head.*   THE MARQUIS *points towards the outside of the palace hidden by the great curtain of the gallery at the back.*

                                On yonder square
A great auto-da-fe takes place in which
A multitude are to be burned alive.
There is an edict also which expels
The Jews, a loyal people whom a monk
Deprives your Highness of.

                        THE KING.
                                A horde we chase,
A crackling stake.   Is this thy great disaster?
   [*He perceives the dish laden with money on the table.*
Whence comes this gold?
   [*To* THE MARQUIS.]   From whom?

                        THE MARQUIS.
                                        The Jews.
                        THE KING.
                                        How much?
                        THE MARQUIS.
The sum amounts to thirty thousand crowns;
It is an offering made in the name
Of thirty cities.

                        THE KING.
         Well, what do they ask?

                        THE MARQUIS.
That they be left in quiet.

                        THE KING.
                        It is much.
I cannot leave in quiet those who still
Continue to be Jews.
                        THE MARQUIS.
                My gracious lord,
Deign to accept this gold a people lays
In fealty at your feet and at your queen's.

They humbly ask their sovereign to forbid
The burning of a hundred of their race.

THE KING.

'T is much.

THE MARQUIS.

A hundred?

THE KING.

No. 'T is much to ask
That I forbid an auto-da-fe. There is
My wife who preaches at me; and there is
The Pope. Both are relentless, and I must
Allow them burn some persons now and then,
Else I should have no peace. What is the news?

THE MARQUIS.

Oh, nothing of importance. Stakes are lit
In Cordova, Tudela, Saragossa.

THE KING.

And nothing further?

THE MARQUIS.

Yes. Count Requesens
One day, when he was drunk, swore by the saints;
His coronet, my liege, did not avail
To save him from the stake in his own town,
Girone. As no lackey had denounced
This nobleman accused of blasphemy,
His household was held guilty, and atoned
By fire and torture for their master's crime.
His very fool was burned.

[GUCHO *leaps up as if startled in his sleep.*

GUCHO (*aside*).

I 'll turn at once
Familiar of the Inquisition! Why,

The devil take me if I don't begin
My work upon the spot. Zounds! burned alive!
A plague upon me, if that's what I want!

    THE KING (*looking at the heap of gold*).
The issue of a bleeding of the Jews;
The race seems made of gold.

    GUCHO (*aside*).
          I am content
To be a looker-on while others roast.

    THE MARQUIS (*to* THE KING).
The Hebrews —
    THE KING.
     Call them Jews!

    THE MARQUIS.
         The Jews, my liege
A numerous, hard-working people, ask,
Prostrate before the King, that he allow them
To live in Spain, nor view with angry eyes
The humble slaves that grovel at his feet.
They ask in fine, my liege, that you revoke
The edict which exiles them.

    THE KING.
        After that,
What do they want?
    THE MARQUIS.
      To die upon the soil
Whereon their fathers died, and to remain
In their own country, sire; and I present
Their ransom. Take it.

    THE KING.
      If the Queen consent,
I will consent. Go beg her to come here.

[*At a sign from* THE KING, GUCHO *goes to the door at the back, and opens it. An officer of the palace appears at the entrance.* GUCHO *speaks to him in a low voice. The officer bows and retires. The door closes.* GUCHO *returns to his former position.*

THE MARQUIS.
The Jews will pass their lives in prayer for you.

THE KING.
It is their money, not their prayers, I want.
Their prayers insult me.

THE MARQUIS.
     Gracious King, your fathers
Liked to reign over them. The Jews exiled,
There is a people less within your realm.

THE KING (*imperiously*).
Enough of this. Much care I for a people!
A girl concerns me more. Since I have shut
That grate between myself and her, I can
No longer sleep. She haunts me in my dreams.
Ah, pshaw! you talk to me of politics,
While I love Rose more madly every day.
My thoughts are all of love. And, by the way,
Has Sancho yet become a monk?

THE MARQUIS.
     Oh, no.
THE KING.
If he refuse, the scaffold is at hand.
I've placed them in two convents in this city,
To have them both within my reach. The girl
Is guarded closely in the Assumption Cloister;

The bars of San Antonio hold the boy.
T was there my ancestor, Don James the Red,
Imprisoned on a time his rebel son.
Don Sancho shall be priest; I'll have the maid,
I will recapture Rose.

     THE MARQUIS.
       And the new edict
Concerning convents?

     THE KING (*astonished*).
      Edict? —

     THE MARQUIS.
         He's declared
A felon, traitor, scoffer of his God,
A parricide accursed, who dares to force
The cloister's sacred doors, or lay a hand
On aught they shelter, though he were yourself.

   THE KING (*gazing fixedly on* THE MARQUIS)
I enter everywhere, and everywhere
I am the King. The moment is at hand
When I shall seize Don Sancho. Though I am
Long suffering, I gain my end at last.
Rose shall be mine.

     THE MARQUIS.
      Ah! but you'll have to deal

     THE KING.
To deal with whom?

     THE MARQUIS.
      But —

     THE KING.
       Speak.

THE MARQUIS.
                            With Torquemada.
THE KING.
What! I, the King!
THE MARQUIS.
          And he the inquisitor!

THE KING.
Ah, pshaw!
THE MARQUIS.
     My liege, in him the Church exists.
If he grow wrathful —
THE KING.
          Well?

THE MARQUIS.
                    The Church lays hold
Of everything with ease, but does not loose
Her grasp with equal readiness. He is
Inquisitor. His office is to see
That convents have their full supply. Nor nun
Nor monk can fraud or force tear from his hands!
He prowls around the cloisters, shows his teeth,
And bites all who approach the tender lambs
This tawny wolf has under watch and ward.
The king who braves the priest, sire, is not wise.
Your path, my liege, is barred by Torquemada.
He checks your course, and all your wrath is vain.

THE KING.
He is a man and easy to corrupt.

THE MARQUIS.
Well, try.

THE KING.

If 't is my wish to tame this monk —

THE MARQUIS.

Sire, try.

THE KING.

I can bestow all man desires.
Before me proudest heads are lowliest bent;
And first, to get the better of a priest,
Why, there are women.

THE MARQUIS.
He is old.

THE KING.

Well, then,
We have the mitre, purple, a grandeeship,
And many dignities and honours.

THE MARQUIS.

Sire,
He will continue monk.

THE KING.
And money.

THE MARQUIS.

Sire,
He will continue poor.

THE KING.

Ah, yes, this man
Is strong, with all the strength of lowliness
And poverty and age.

[THE KING *crosses his arms and muses*
Close by myself
To feel that sombre poverty which casts
A shadow on my throne! which, in its power,
Stands on a level with the king!

THE MARQUIS.
       Ay, higher!
THE KING.
No!
THE MARQUIS.
 Women, honours, gold are powerless
Against this monk.
THE KING.
      I could find other means.
Dost understand?
THE MARQUIS.
     No. Which?
THE KING.
        The right ones, eh?
Dost understand?
THE MARQUIS.
     No.

THE KING.
      Why, old Arbuez
Was stabbed upon the very altar steps.
Was not that system good?

THE MARQUIS.
       It turned out bad.
Old Arbuez became Saint Arbuez,
And that was all. You reign, and you allot
Domains and dignities, or, if you will,
The headsman's axe. But with the hand that tries
To hold the Church, she strives with fiery zeal.
You persecute her and you make her stronger.
The priests have this distinctive quality, —
That when you kill them, they 're the more alive.
They never disappear. From hecatombs
Springs into life that spectral form. the priest.

Their blood's eternal, and their bones are fruitful.
We crush them living, we invoke them dead.
Ah, sire! you think to break the Church's power.
She bursts at once her bonds by palms and hymns,
By tears and martyrdom. Yes, massacre
The cloister's hypocrite, with malice drunk!
Strike! It is well. Now raise to heaven your eyes.
'T is filled with saints of your own making, sire!
Fold reverent hands and fall upon your knees.
I do admire the Church. For, slave or queen,
She has the final say. She swarms below
Here on this earth; she swarms in heaven above,
And crushed as vermin, rises as a star.

THE KING (*depressed*).

She's the disease, and I am the diseased.
Thou sayest truth. Brave Rome, and you repent.
We must resign ourselves.

THE MARQUIS (*aside*).

What does he mean?
The danger with him is that if you want
A certain course to be pursued by him
You must advise the opposite, and if
You wish him to go north, you needs must urge
His footsteps towards the south. This time I see
That he believes my words. My ruse has failed!
The tortuous path that I have found so useful
Avails not here. I must aim at my goal,
And change my style.
[*Aloud.*] Ah! you have let the monk
Grow all too great, and now he has become
Of monstrous size.

THE KING (*musing*).

This Torquemada —

THE MARQUIS.

                            Sire,
Holds Spain. He is her Pontiff, and where'er
You lay your finger-nail he puts his claw.
He fills your seat. Ah! sire, the time is past
When at your royal pleasure you might go
Into a convent, and with threatening frown
Compel this stubborn Church to own your power.
You then might hang a monk. You dare not touch
His frock at present. Ah, your monk's a trial!
Your gibbets! Strike the priests! Attempt it, sire!
Your laws have everything to fear from his;
And surely he would laugh to see a fight
Between your scaffold and his fiery stake.
The duel is unequal. Sire, the earth
Owns as its lord this monk; and as wild oats
Are set on fire by peasants, living men
Are turned to ashes by his flaming torch.
The palaces appalled like cloisters look;
On every side the clergy sprouts and grows
Like brier and bramble. Everything gives way
Before the frowning monk. "The devil take
The hindmost" is the cry. The proudest crawl,
The bravest tremble. What, my liege, is done
From Cadiz to Tortosa through your realm?
Your subjects are denouncing one another,
Two cousins of your Highness are in chains,
The Marquis Alfonzo and Prince of Viana,
And that coarse hand has even been laid upon
The Infante of Tudela. Lately gay
Was every town and village in our Spain;
To-day a pall of silence over all.
No more the innocent laugh, no more the feast,
A banquet is suspected. Terror, fear,
And mourning reign in all parts of our land,

And this huge Spain is like a festival
When all the lights are quenched.   Your forests, sire
Are used for scaffolds ; wood begins to fail.
Crimes true and false are intermingled.   All
Is good to feed the fagots.   You have seen
Some one pass by you, you are his accomplice.
A son betrays his father, father son.
Who, unaware, lets fall a crucifix
Is burned alive.   A word, a gesture, is
A heresy.   This horrible monk has looked
On Jesus with a madman's eye.   All acts
Are heinous crimes.   To swear by Solomon,
To have the air of whispering to the devil,
To pare the nails, go barefoot on fast days,
To wed a wife that's too old or too young,
To turn a corpse's face towards the wall,
Or not to fly before those who bind tight
Their loins with leathern cord, to lay a cloth
Upon one's table on a Saturday,
To drive the ox at Christmas from the stable,
To name God oftener than Jesus, or
To hide one's self, — all these lead to the stake.
Repeating verses in a funeral train,
Or weeping, in the shade, behind a door,
Or watching in some lonely desert spot
The rising of night's earliest star, — these, too,
Are crimes.   These blazing piles devour, O King,
And mount and ever mount, and more and more
With this red dawn empurple all the sky
Above you, sire.   It is your subjects' blood
Which you are robbed of.   Soon you shall not have
The soldiers which your wars require.   Just now —
But what avail my words ! the King cares not, —
The King, who by a word could change it all.
But no ! — The Holy Office lately placed

All Spain within a padded cell, and it
Has come to pass your subjects scarcely know you.
[*He points to the gallery at the back and the curtain which
closes it.* GUCHO *is listening attentively.*
This very day, O King, beneath your window
A monstrous pile of fire will flame to heaven,
And there beneath the gaze of wanton eyes
Shall women turn and writhe clad but with flame.
At the four corners statues will arise, —
Four huge, black prophets built of hollow stone,
And full of living men, — Colossuses,
Whose hideous bellowing will be heard around.
The shuddering fire will lick their open mouths,
And at the end naught but these giants stand.
Your people, haggard, horror-stricken, see
You and your kingdoms vanish in the smoke
That wraps up these four phantoms; for all light
Comes from the hateful Quemadero. Sire,
You disappear when you're surrounded by
The shadow of the executioner.

[THE KING *sits down on a folding-stool, overwhelmed.*

THE KING.

All this is for the Church's gain.

THE MARQUIS.
      And for
The kingdom's loss. Castile with charnel houses
Is covered. Far and near rise cries of fright.
      [*Drawing near to* THE KING.
Alas! you struggle vainly. You are caught.
Above your Spain is stretched a sombre web,
Through which you may see God, like some vague star;
A gloomy net, that Satan fixed to earth
And spun out, thread by thread, from Jehovah's bowels;

A snare in which the wretched human mind
Is spent and broken; an immense rose-window,
Belonging to an infinite church, through which
The light of hell on the high altar gleams.
There shudder horror, night, and deadly fear;
And earth regards with woful eyes that thing
Which it has ever o'er it in the dark.
It dreams of that old Baal in whose clasp
It erstwhile stifled. To grow great is wrong;
To think, a grievous sin; to live is boldness.
Existence is a peril. At the centre
Of that dark web is seen the priest, that spider,
And always, close by him, that fly, the King.
[THE KING *bends his head.* THE MARQUIS *watches him
and continues.*

Faith, it is strange and terrible as well
That out of that vile yarn, vows, cloister, rule,
And dogma, there should spring a web so vast
That it could snare an eagle; but 't is done.
The eagle's caught, and at the present hour
Gives but one little tremble of his wing
Within the net. Before you threatening stand
The missal, Bible, gospel; and for you
To will is an impossibility,
To love you dare not; you dare reign no longer.
The kings of old, hard as the mountain rock,
And long-haired as the woods, had prouder thoughts.
Ah, well! the present is, more than the past,
But dust. A maiden's beauty wins a king.
This gentle sovereign crawls along, nor tries
A single royal roar. There is no more
Aught great upon the earth except the priest;
And he, this monk — oh, why do children dare
Come into life! — this monk is King. He has
Beneath his sandals you! He drives the bolts

Upon the human soul. He's greater far
Than bishop or than abbess in the eyes
Of deacon or of nun.   He comes; the law
Bows down before him.   Lowly, like a reed,
The sceptre bends.   The sword is terrified.
His fixed eyes a boundless stupor spread.
Man is his target, empire is his goal,
And this dark spy of God, who throws o'er all
His terrible shadow, ambushes the world.
     [*Looking* THE KING *in the face.*
A time will come when history shall say:
" It was the age of fire.   It was the time
Of slavery and darkness.   Its great work ? —
'T was ashes; and a fork to stir the embers
Replaced the sceptre once Pelagio held.
The name borne by the monarch ?   Torquemada."

    THE KING (*rising*).

Thou liest, Marquis, in thy throat.   His name
Was Ferdinand, and neither monk nor Pope
Shall bring to pass that it be otherwise,
Or that I be not King, — I, who am both
The tiger and the lion! and I'll prove
My kingly state by cutting off some heads.
Go, get me men, and see they have their swords;
Then straightway to the Assumption Convent march,
And seize the Infanta.   Smite all who resist;
'T is my good pleasure.   Let all bend the knee,
And be reduced to utter nothingness,
As much before you as if on a sudden
They had beheld my face!   And now the order.
[*He approaches the table, takes a pen and sheet of parchment, and writes rapidly.*
"Submit, it is the law.   Whatever act
The Marquis does, it is willed by the King."
  [*He signs and hands the parchment to* THE MARQUIS.

And if there be resistance, smite, destroy,
Burn, crush, exterminate, and leave no man
Alive, or standing wall when you have quit
The cursed spot on which that convent stood.
    [GUCHO *is listening with more attention than ever.*

THE MARQUIS.
And if some monk should —

THE KING.
                Death!
THE MARQUIS.
                      Or trooper?
THE KING.
                            Chain
A hundred cut-throats of my African guard
Take with you. You'll find they're enough to force
The barriers of one convent.

THE MARQUIS (*aside*).
                    And of two.
[*Aloud.*]   Although it has the sanction of the King,
This stroke is hazardous, my gracious liege.

THE KING.
Ah, pshaw!
THE MARQUIS.
        When I have taken the Infanta,
I must conceal her somewhere.

THE KING.
                    Surely.
THE MARQUIS.
                        Where?
THE KING.
Within my private park. 'T is dark and lonely.
You know I leave this evening?

THE MARQUIS.
Yes, I know.
But for a day.
THE KING.
I journey to Triana.
On my return I would wish to find
The Infanta in —
THE MARQUIS.
The private park?
THE KING.
Yes, there.
I 'm master.
THE MARQUIS.
But the key?
[THE KING *goes to the sideboard, and opens a drawer.*
I 've two, for I
Alone can enter there.
[*He takes out two keys, and hands one to* THE MARQUIS.
I give you one.
[*He puts the other in the drawer, which he pushes back. When* THE KING'S *back is turned,* GUCHO *creeps under the different articles of furniture, opens the drawer again, and takes out the key which* THE KING *has just placed there.*
GUCHO (*aside*).
I take the other.
[*He shuts the drawer, and thrusts the key in his pocket.*

THE KING.
Ah! the monks are strong,
The priests are great! Ah! Torquemada reigns!
Well, we shall see.
[*The voice of an Usher, outside, announcing:*
The Queen, our sovereign Lady.

[*Enter* THE QUEEN, *all in jet-black, with the royal crown on her head. She makes a profound reverence to* THE KING, *who returns it, without taking off his cap.* THE QUEEN *proceeds to one of the arm-chairs at the extremity of the table and sits down; then remains motionless, as if she neither saw nor heard anything.* THE KING *and* THE QUEEN *have each a rosary at the girdle.*

THE KING (*in a low voice to* THE MARQUIS).
Make haste; for speed is vital to success.
Go, Marquis, do what I have bid thee do.
[*Enter* THE DUKE OF ALAVA. *He proceeds towards* THE KING.
What is it, Duke?

THE DUKE (*after saluting* THE KING *and* QUEEN).
    The deputies, my liege,
Sent by the Jews you banish from your realm,
Sue for the favour, gracious King and Queen,
Of lying prostrate at your Highness' feet.

THE KING.
'T is granted. Let them enter.   [THE DUKE *leaves*
[*In a low voice to* THE MARQUIS.] Run at once
To the Assumption Convent, and lay hold
Of the Infanta.

THE MARQUIS (*aside*).
   Then to San Antonio.

THE KING.
Away!

THE MARQUIS.
  But—

THE KING.
What?

THE MARQUIS.
If the Inquisitor? —

THE KING.
That monk indeed! He is the earthworm, and
The dragon I.

SCENE III.

THE KING, THE QUEEN, THE JEWS.

*Through the door at the back, wide open, come a frightened
and ragged crowd between two rows of halberds and
pikes. They are the deputies of the Jews, men, women,
and children, all covered with ashes and in tattered
clothes, barefooted, with ropes about their necks. Some,
mutilated and enfeebled by torture, drag themselves
along on crutches or stumps; others, deprived of their
eyes, are led by children. At their head is the Grand
Rabbi,* MOSES-BEN-HABIB. *All have the yellow badge
prescribed for their race on their torn apparel. At
some distance from the table,* THE RABBI *stops and
falls on his knees. All behind him prostrate themselves.
The old men strike the floor with their foreheads.
Neither* THE KING *nor* THE QUEEN *looks at them.
They seem to be gazing at vacancy, above all these heads.*

THE RABBI (*on his knees*).
Your Highness of Castile,
Of Aragon, our sovereign King and Queen!
Your trembling subjects are in sore distress,
And, praying first to God, we come to you,

With naked feet and rope about our necks,
And bring our groans and tears to you, O Kings!
For we are lying in death's very shadow,
A number of us are about to be
Flung on the fagots, and for all the rest,
Old men and women, exile is decreed.
Your edicts, King and Queen, o'erwhelm us all.
We weep, our fathers shudder in their graves, —
You cause the mournful sepulchres to tremble.
Be merciful. Our hearts are meek and true.
Shut up within our little homes, we live
Alone and humble. All our laws are plain, —
So very simple that a little child
Might set them down in writing. Never Jew
Is seen to sing or laugh. We pay the tribute;
We never ask how large the sum may be.
We're trod upon while lying on the ground;
We're like the garment of a murdered man.
To God be glory! But must Israel
Defenceless, driving ox and ass and dog
Before him, flee, dispersed in every sense,
With new-born suckling babes and children weaned!
Must we ne'er be a people, wanderers ever!
O King and Queen, do not let us be chased
With goad of pike, and God for you shall open
Celestial gates. Have mercy on us. We
Are dashed to earth. Shall we no longer see
Our trees and fields of corn? Shall mothers have
No longer milk within their breasts? The beasts
Are in the forests, happy with their mates;
The nests sleep calmly, couched beneath the leaves;
The hind brings up her little ones in peace.
Ah! let us also live within our caves,
Beneath our squalid roofs. For there we dwell
Almost like slaves within a convict pen,

But near our fathers' graves. In mercy deign
To suffer us to rest beneath your feet
Which we have bathed with tears! Alas! the woe
Of wandering along the distant ways!
Then let us drink the waters of our streams,
And live upon our fields, and prosperous days
Shall wait upon your steps. Alas! we wring
Our hands in desperation. Spare us, Kings,
The agony of exile, and the dole
Of stern, eternal, endless loneliness!
Grant us our country, grant our native skies!
The bread we eat with tears is bitter bread.
Be not the wind, though we be but the dust.
                       [Pointing to the gold on the table.
Behold our ransom. Deign to take it, Kings,
And, oh! protect us. Look on our despair.
Be angels o'er us, but not angels dark,
But angels good and mild. The shadow cast
By gloomy wings is not the same, O Kings,
As that the white wing leaves. Recall your ban.
We beg it in the name of those great kings,
Your sacred ancestors, the lion-hearted,
And by the tombs of sovereigns august,
Who shone serene in wisdom's light. We place
Our hearts, O rulers of the human race,
Our prayers, our sorrows in the little hands
Of Joan, the Infanta, innocent
And like unto the wildwood strawberry
Where lights the bee. O King, O Queen, have mercy!
[*A moment of silence. Absolute impassiveness of* THE
  KING *and* QUEEN. *Neither turns the eye.* THE DUKE
  OF ALAVA, *who is standing before the table with naked
  sword, touches the shoulder of* THE GRAND RABBI *with
  the flat.* THE GRAND RABBI *rises, and with the other
  Jews, retires backward with head bent down. The*

guards form a line and force them back. The door remains open after they leave. THE KING *beckons to* THE DUKE OF ALAVA, *who approaches.*

THE KING (*to* THE DUKE).

The Queen and I would privately discuss
The edict. Duke, arrest whoever comes,
Although he be a prince. Whoever dares
To enter here shall surely lose his head.
Go, close the door, and guard the passage well.
[THE DUKE *lowers his sword, bows, raises his sword again, and goes. The two leaves of the door shut.* THE KING *and* QUEEN *are alone. During this scene* GUCHO *has disappeared under the tapestry that covers the table, where he is concealed.*

SCENE IV.

THE KING, THE QUEEN, GUCHO *under the table.* THE KING *and* QUEEN *regard each other earnestly and silently for a time. At last* THE QUEEN *lowers her eyes and looks at the money on the table.*

THE QUEEN.

A sum of thirty thousand marks of gold.

THE KING.

A sum of thirty thousand marks of gold.

THE QUEEN.

But they are an accursed race, and all
Star-gazers.

THE KING.

        Thirty thousand marks of gold
Make up six hundred thousand piasters,
And that is twenty million sequins.

THE QUEEN.

                              Sequins?

THE KING.

Yes, sequins, which, to Moorish besants changed,
Would make enough to load a galley, Queen!

THE QUEEN.

But still a Jew becomes invisible
By lighting fingers of a buried child.

THE KING.

'T is true, no doubt.

THE QUEEN.

                They would a vessel load?

THE KING.

Ay, to the very deck.

THE QUEEN.

        With besants?

THE KING.

                      Yes,
And changed to silver douros, we would have
In weight as much again.

THE QUEEN.

           My mind's confused,
Suppose we said a pater?
[*She takes her rosary. A moment of silence.* THE KING
   touches the piles of gold and stirs them.

THE KING (*in an undertone*).
                      With this gold
I might without expense on Boabdil
Make war.

THE QUEEN (*all the time telling her beads*).
          If I should be the first to die,
Swear to me, sir, to take no other wife.

THE KING (*in an undertone*).
Yes, with this gold make war —

THE QUEEN.
                     Will you not swear?

THE KING.
Swear what? — Oh, yes, of course.
               [*Musing*] This gold would pay
For all expenses, all. Granada would
Be ours, a jewel in our diadem.
[THE QUEEN, *having finished her prayers, places the rosary on the table.*

THE QUEEN.
Sir, let us take the gold, and, all the same,
Exile the Jews, whom I cannot accept
As subjects.
[THE KING *raises his head.* THE QUEEN *speaks more strongly.*
          Then let us exile the Jews
And keep their money.

THE KING.
              I was thinking of it.
But such a deed might well discourage others
From acting like the Jews.

THE QUEEN (*looking at the money*).
                With all this gold!
And in your hands —
                THE KING.
                In yours.

                THE QUEEN.
                        Might more be asked?
                THE KING.
Well, later on.
                [*He handles the piles of gold.*
                Granada I could wrest
From the vile bastard crescent. Though we kept
The Jews, yet still we might expel the Moors.

                THE QUEEN (*wavering*).
'T is true.
                THE KING.
        A compensation.

                THE QUEEN.
                        Yes, a choice
Between Gomorrahs.

                THE KING.
                Then do we accept
The money?
                THE QUEEN.
        Yes.
[*He takes a pen and writes some lines on a parchment, after consulting* THE QUEEN *by a look.*

                THE KING.
                Well, then. "The edict is
Annulled which banishes that miscreant tribe,
The Jews, and parts them from the Spanish people;

It is forbid to light the stake prepared;
'T is ordered that imprisoned Jews be freed."
[THE KING *signs, then hands the pen and parchment to*
    THE QUEEN.

     THE QUEEN (*taking the pen*).
'T is settled.
[*Just as* THE QUEEN *is about to sign, the great door opens
    with much noise.* THE KING *and* QUEEN *turn around
    in amazement.* GUCHO *thrusts out his head.* TORQUE-
    MADA *appears on the threshold in his Dominican robe
    and with an iron crucifix in his hand.*

SCENE V.

THE KING, THE QUEEN, TORQUEMADA. TORQUEMADA
looks neither at THE KING *nor* THE QUEEN. *He has
his eyes fixed on the crucifix.*

     TORQUEMADA.
  Once for thirty silver pieces
Did Judas sell thee; now this King and Queen
Sell thee for thirty thousand golden crowns.

     THE QUEEN.
O Heaven!

 TORQUEMADA (*casting the crucifix on the pile of gold*).
   Advance, and seize him, Jews!

     THE QUEEN.
         Good father!
     TORQUEMADA.
Rejoice, ye Jews! this King and Queen, as it
Is writ, deliver to you Jesus Christ.

THE QUEEN.

My father!

TORQUEMADA (*looking them both in the face*).
King, be thou accursed! be thou
Accursed, O Queen!

THE QUEEN.
Forgiveness!

TORQUEMADA (*stretching his arm above them*).
On your knees!
[THE QUEEN *falls on her knees;* THE KING *hesitates trembling.*
Both! [THE KING *falls on his knees*
[*Pointing to* ISABEL.] On this side, the Queen.
[*Pointing to* FERDINAND.] On that, the King.
A pile of gold between. Ah! you are king,
And you are queen!
[*He seizes the crucifix, and raises it high above his head.*
And this is God. Behold!
I have surprised you in the very act,
Red-handed. Kiss the ground.

THE QUEEN (*prostrating herself*).
Forgive us, father!

TORQUEMADA.

Oh, horror!

THE QUEEN.
Give us absolution, father!

TORQUEMADA.

Measureless insolence! — It is thy reign,
O Antichrist, at last! The Jews restored!

The auto-da-fe proscribed! The helpful stake
To be no longer lit! These sovereigns
Forbid it. So, that wretch, the sceptre, dares
To touch the cross! The prince, that bandit, dares
To close his ears to all that Christ hath said!
The time has come when ye must be forewarned.
The Holy Office has its rights o'er you.
The Pope alone's exempt from its decrees,
But kings are not. Our banner has the right
To go into your palaces, proud Kings!
At every hour, e'en while you sleep or eat,
And with it bring its melancholy doom!
Kings, those false gods, have ever been the aim
At which the thunderbolts of Heaven are hurled,
For Heaven hates kings. O princes, all your laws
Are vain and worthless. Ours alone are true:
We are the wheat, and you the tares. Some day
The reaper's scythe shall cut enormous swaths!
Kings, we endure you, but denounce your crimes.
Each day into the gulf we cast your names
Where dark and lonely pangs await your advent!
The floors of hell are paved with skulls of kings.
Ah, yes! because your ports are filled with sails,
Because your soldiers throng your camps, you think
That you are strong. God with quiescent eye
Amid the stars is meditating. Tremble.

THE QUEEN.

Forgive!

THE KING (*rising*).

My lord inquisitor, the King
And Queen, with contrite heart, and as a sign
Of their devotion to the faith, intend
Repairing wrongs they were about to do.
The Jews shall be expelled; and we, besides,

Empower you, father, and the Holy Office,
And all your holy priests to light at once
The stake.

TORQUEMADA.

And do you think I waited?

[*He descends the three steps, goes to the gallery at the back, and violently draws the curtain aside.*

Look!

[*Night is beginning to fall. Through the wide, open lattice at the back of the gallery, the square of La Tablada is seen covered with an immense crowd. In the centre of the square is the Quemadero. An enormous piece of masonry all bristling with flames, filled with stakes and posts, and with those condemned in sanbenitos, who are seen through the smoke. Barrels of lighted pitch are nailed to the tops of the posts, and empty in flames on the heads of the condemned. Women, whom the fire has rendered naked, are burning, fastened to piles. Cries are heard. At the four corners of the Quemadero are four gigantic statues, called the four Evangelists, reddened by the blaze. They have holes and openings through which are seen men howling and arms writhing like living brands. The whole has a terrific aspect of torture and conflagration.* THE KING *and* THE QUEEN *look on appalled.* GUCHO, *under the table, stretches his neck and tries to see.* TORQUEMADA, *in meditation, sates his eyes with the Quemadero.*

TORQUEMADA.

O festival of glory and of joy!
O grand and terrible clemency of flames!
Deliverance forever! O ye damned!
Ye are absolved! The stake on earth hath quenched
The hell below. O blessed stake, by which
The soul mounts up! Thou honourest the fire,

The shame of hell. O outlet bordering on
The radiant pathway, gate of paradise,
Once more reopened for the human race!
O ardent pity with thy numberless
Caresses, mystic ransom of hell's slaves.
Auto da-fe! thou 'rt pardon, kindness, light,
And fire and life! a dazzling splendour on
The face of God! Oh, what a grand demise!
What souls are saved! Jews, sinners, infidels, —
Ah, my dear children, one brief, sudden pang
Rewards you with eternal happiness;
Man is no more accursed, no more exiled.
Salvation opens in the depths of heaven.
Love wakes, and yonder is his wondrous triumph!
What ecstasy! to enter heaven at once!
Not languish by the way! [*Cries heard from the stakes.*
     Hear ye the howls
Of Satan as he sees them all escape?
Let the eternal felon weep and wail
In his eternal den. With these two hands
I 've pushed his huge red door. Oh, how he gnashed,
When on him I made fast those hideous leaves,
Forever, Never! And the Wicked One
Remains behind the sombre wall. [*He looks up to the sky.*
    Oh, I
Have healed the grisly wound his shadow made.
Ah! paradise was maimed; and in the side
Of heaven was that ulcer, burning hell,
Ensanguined hell; o'er hell I 've placed the flame,
The healing flame, and as mine eyes behold
The boundless sky, I see the cicatrice.
It was the spear-thrust in thy side, O Christ!
Hosanna! the eternal wound is cured.
     [*He looks at the Quemadero.*
Ye rubies of the flame! Ye precious stones

Of fiery coals! Blaze up, ye brands! burn, embers!
O sovran fire, beam brightly! shine, O stake!
Thou casket of bright sparks soon to be stars!
The soul, freed from the body's vesture, flies,
And from the bath of torments bliss comes forth!
O splendour! fierce magnificence of flame!
Ha! Satan, my black foe, what sayest thou?
[*In an esctasy.*] O fire, thou washest all foul stains away!
Supreme transfiguration! act of faith!
We are two fork-bearers, the Fiend and I,
Two masters of the flames. I succour souls,
And he is man's destroyer. We are both
Two executioners, and by like means
We make — one, heaven, and the other, hell;
He makes the evil, and I make the good;
He's in the sewer, in the temple I;
And the black quivering shadow views us both.
                    [*He turns again to the condemned.*
O dear, beloved brethren! but for me
You all were lost. You now are cleansed from sin
In that piscina by its writhing flames.
Ah! for the passing moment you will curse me;
But ah! dear children! you will give me thanks
When you behold from what you have escaped;
Because, like Michael the archangel, I
Have also slain; because white seraphim,
Who stoop above the pit of sulphur, mock
The marvellous miscarriage of the gulf;
Because your howls of hatred in the light
Shall stammer, and, in stupefaction, end
In songs of love! Alas! what pangs were mine
To see you in the torture chambers lie,
With wails and tears and shrieks and writhing limbs!
To see you by the vice and pincers torn!
But now you're free! Depart! ascend to heaven!

Pass into paradise!
[*He stoops and seems to be looking at something beneath the earth.*

No, thou shalt have
No longer souls! [*He stands erect.*
The Lord hath given us
The help we asked, and man's freed from the gulf.
Depart! away! across the burning gloom
And through the great winged flames, the whirling smoke
Bears to the skies the living spirit saved
From the dead flesh! and all old human crimes
Are torn up by the roots. One had his sins,
Another had his errors, fault or vice;
Each soul had in itself a monster who
Would nibble at its light and champ its wings.
The angel faded fast, the demon's prey.
Now all is burned, and by the light of tombs,
And in the presence of our Saviour Christ,
The radiant and august division's made.
Fall into dust, ye dragons! Take your flight,
Ye doves! For you whom hell had in its grip
'T is liberty! From darkness mount to light!
For time take in exchange eternity!

ACT III.

SCENE. — *It is night. A terrace of the private park, called Huerto del Rey in Seville. The terrace is broad. It communicates on the left and right with alleys of trees. At the back it is crossed by a staircase, the steps of which are not seen, by which the terrace is reached from the garden. Only the top of the head is first seen of those who arrive on the terrace by this staircase, then the body gradually comes into view, until they are on a level with the terrace. On the terrace is a bench of marble. The lower part of the garden is lost in obscurity. The moon is rising during the act.*

SCENE I.

TORQUEMADA, GUCHO. *They enter by the alley on the right, GUCHO conducting TORQUEMADA. GUCHO presses his two bawbles against his breast with one hand, and with the other presents a key to TORQUEMADA.*

GUCHO.

Deign to remember that 't is I who give
The key of the King's private park to you, —
I, Gucho, fool of the said King, our sire.
What crime are they about? I cannot tell.
I 'm all at sea, and find it better far
That you be here to see with your own eyes.
The cloister's sacred rights are put in peril;
Likewise a maiden whom the King would force,
Although she was betrothed to his young cousin,
With the consent of all her family:
'T is all I know about this wicked plot.
I am the king's buffoon, my lord; 't is I
Who make him laugh, — that is, when he 's inclined.

[TORQUEMADA *takes the key from the hand of* GUCHO.

GUCHO (*aside*).

Denunciation's bad; but to be grilled! —
Ugh! it is worse. My choice is made. Oh, thank you!
I was not born with a silver spoon,
And do not count on bettering my fate
By shining in an auto-da-fe, my friend.
Shine, by all means, but as a wit, not candle.
The question is to whom I'm faithful now.
Why, to myself. You gaby, did you think
I was a hero or some dashing knight,
Or surly, stubborn fellow, bent to be
A martyr? You have made a great mistake.
What will occur? Of that I wash my paws.
Besides, I hardly think the King would die
Of grief if I were roasted. Yon old fellow
Has but to raise his finger, and his Highness
Plumps flat upon his belly. Then, denounce,
I say. Why not? Think only of yourself.
I'm devilish sure to get out of a scrape,
And sheer away, I tell you!

TORQUEMADA (*regarding the key, aside*).
      Coward King!
Both vile and wicked. Scarce is he absolved
When he begins again.
[GUCHO *has gone to the back of the terrace. He gives a look
  into the obscure depths of the garden.*

GUCHO (*aside*).
     I see a group
Beneath a tree. It looks as if they were
About to mount the marble staircase. There
Are three! Why three? Oh, leave aside the why,
Let everything behind me go to smash,
If I get off scot-free!

TORQUEMADA (*aside, looking at the garden*).
                            So this, then, is
The secret park, the shelter of his vices.
    [*He walks with slow steps into the alley on his left.*

        GUCHO (*aside, looking down the staircase*).
Ah! here is some one coming. I am off.
[*He leaves by the side he entered.* THE MARQUIS DE FUENTAL *is seen coming up first; then* DON SANCHO *and* DONNA ROSE *appear, both in the habit of novices, as in the first act.* THE MARQUIS *conducts them with his finger on his lips. He looks around him cautiously.*

SCENE II.

THE MARQUIS DE FUENTAL, DON SANCHO, DONNA ROSE.

THE MARQUIS.

Your novice garb, if it were day, would be
A peril. But 't is night, the place is lonely,
None see us. O great God! You 're free at last,
And not a soul suspects that you are here.
I did not take the usual path, and so
I was not followed. I have sent away
The people I employed. I tremble, still,
For nothing is secure. We must have clothes
And horses, and we must take flight at once.
All should be ready ere the morning dawns.
            [*Looking down the lonely alleys of the park.*
Oh! I made fast the gate. No danger there.
The King alone can enter. He 's away.
[*To* DON SANCHO.] Confide in me, my prince, and trust
    me, Madame;
To free you from your prisons cost me much.

To save you next will be a frightful task;
But yet I am resolved, and feel my strength
Increase before the peril. To you both
I consecrate my life. The first step was
To take you from the convent, and the next
Must be to take you out of Spain. Alas!
My mind is fertile in resources. Yet
To pass across the frontier how shall we
Devise a plan? This Torquemada holds
All Spain within his grasp, and of the King's
Abasement makes his greatness. I have forced
Two convents, and the Grand Inquisitor
Will surely track my footsteps. Here, so far,
We are untroubled. But before the dawn
We must seek out some other refuge, for
The King may come. Alas! what shall we do?
Where find a person who would shelter you
And wish to save you? Yes, some monk alone
Could do it. Priests are now all-powerful;
I'll search for one. But no, they're traitors all,
And sometimes sell those who have purchased them.
Oh! how I wish you safely placed in France!
There is another source of fear, besides,
I cannot hide from you. This private park,
Although it is a lonely spot, is near
The palace of the Holy Office. Nay,
The rampart that surrounds it meets the wall
That girds the prisons of the Inquisition.
I leave you for a moment. Do we fly
Or die together? Yes! I go to seek
A refuge for you. Ah! I tremble. Still,
You are alive. God guard you!

DON SANCHO.
'T is to you
That we owe all!

THE MARQUIS.

             O my poor banished friends,
I must find means to baffle your pursuers.
Await me here.

DON SANCHO.
           How can we thank you, say?

THE MARQUIS.

By being happy.
[*He goes out in the same direction in which* GUCHO *has gone.*

SCENE III.

DON SANCHO, DONNA ROSE.

DON SANCHO.
                     Ah! I quake with fear.
To see thee once again is heaven; but
To tremble for thee, ah! what dread despair!

DONNA ROSE.

God joins us. God will save us too.
            [*She gazes on him with rapture.*
                I love thee!
[*They rush passionately into each other's arms*

DON SANCHO (*gazing at the sky*).

Oh! why from yonder starry heights does no
Immortal being swoop through air, and cast
His shadow over thee? Has heaven no more
Its angels, or, alas! have angels now
No longer wings?

DONNA ROSE.
We have a faithful friend
In this poor man.
DON SANCHO.
Alas! he is himself
Dismayed. On every side there's danger.
[TORQUEMADA *appears. He is among the trees in darkness. He has heard these last words. He is listening and gazing. He watches* DON SANCHO *and* DONNA ROSE *with a sort of increasing surprise. They do not see him.* DON SANCHO *takes the hand of* DONNA ROSE *and raises his eyes to heaven.*

                                              Oh!
Who then is likely to protect thee?

TORQUEMADA.
I!
[*Both turn round in amazement.*

SCENE IV.

DON SANCHO, DONNA ROSE, TORQUEMADA.

TORQUEMADA.
I know you now.
DONNA ROSE.
It is the aged monk!

TORQUEMADA.
I am the man Gomorrah had condemned
And Sodom struck; but for your aid, my children,
I was within the sepulchre. You came,

My stranger friends, and gave me freedom. You,
The dove and eagle, dragged me from the tomb.
To you I owe to see the light of day.
Ah! you have saved me, now it is my turn!

DONNA ROSE.

Yes, 't is the monk!

TORQUEMADA.

Your robes of serge declare
That to the Virgin both are consecrate.
I find you such as when I saw you first.
I was no longer living, though not dead;
You came like two bright angels from on high,
And saved me. God in marvellous ways to-day
Has led me on your road. You cry for help,
I stretch you out my hand. God has employed
Saint Dominick to watch the conduct of
Pedro the Second; me, of Ferdinand,
That guilty prince. I heard you as I passed.
You seem in peril. Are you prisoners, then?
What succour do you need? God gained for me,
Some duty to perform, I knew not what,
An entrance into this suspicious place,
This cavern dark. I find you grieving here,
Nor am surprised, since God conducts us both,
And, step by step, guides you and me. I was
Within the tomb. You came. Now, captives too,
You tremble in this dismal spot. I come.
Without me you would perish. But for you
I was destroyed. As you were unforeseen,
So I am unexpected. Wherefore, then,
Have you come hither? Wherefore in your fate
Have I a part? You were the miracle,
I am the wonder. God knows what he does.

SANCHO (*to* DONNA ROSE).

'T is he!

TORQUEMADA.

No longer fear, for I am there.
I have a dim perception of some plot.
Recluse and monk, I yet know what men are.
I love you, and I will defend you 'gainst
The King himself.

DON SANCHO.

You are, then, near the King?

TORQUEMADA.

Above.

DON SANCHO.

Pray, who, then, are you?

TORQUEMADA.

Nothing by
Myself; by Jesus everything.

DON SANCHO.

Your name?

TORQUEMADA.

My name's Deliverance. I am he who through
The dread transparency of earth beholds
The hell beneath, and all the devils of hell
Whom, haggard and dismayed, my gaze pursues;
And I perceive the bottom of that gulf
Which all must fear, — that sombre, awful fire;
And I possess the urn shall quench its flames.
But tell me, you — how do men call you?

DON SANCHO.

Sancho
Infante of Burgos.

DONNA ROSE.
And Rose, Infanta
Of Orthez.

DON SANCHO.
We're betrothed.

TORQUEMADA.
You have but ta'en
The vows a dispensation may annul.
How comes it you are here?

DON SANCHO.
The King by force
Has put me in a convent; also her.
We fled.

TORQUEMADA.
For which you'll pay a fine. The King
Shall pay at higher rate. His fault has been
A graver one. It is a crime to make
God's Holy Place the prison of the King,
And no one goes into a convent but
Of his own wish. You're free. Be hopeful, Rose!
Have courage, Sancho! What do you wish more?

DON SANCHO.
To marry, father.

TORQUEMADA.
I am well content,
And I will marry you myself.

DONNA ROSE.
My lord!
[*She is about to throw herself at his feet.* TORQUEMADA *by a gesture, prevents her.*

TORQUEMADA.

Unto the dead, the joys of Paradise;
Unto the living, happiness: it is
That which I bring, who, calm and humble, hold
A torch and palm in either hand. May you
Be happy!

DON SANCHO.

Oh, what bliss! I know not why,
When I 'm near you, I fear no more the King.
If I feared any one, it would be you!
You are like some strange providence above
Our heads, at once tremendous and supreme.

TORQUEMADA.

Like Rachel, who saw Jacob and did wed,
The patriarch, Rose, you shall be the bride
Of Sancho, and the grace of God will foil
The projects of this King, which I divine.
Yes, I shall save you both. Depend on me.

DONNA ROSE.

Whoever you may be, priest, bishop, thanks!
May Heaven's choicest blessings on you fall!
O saintly father, 't was a sacred hour
When God permitted us to hear your cry
Within the tomb!

DON SANCHO.

I seem to see it all:
It was a lovely April day, and I
Was gathering roses, she was running after
The butterflies, the words we whispered low
Were blended with the sunlight; evening came,
When suddenly I hear a cry. 'T was like
A call for help from some one dying; then
I see a stone, and listen —

DONNA ROSE.

      And you said:
"A man is underneath! Come, let us save him!"
But, then, the stone too heavy was, alas!

DON SANCHO.

And, Rose, a cross of iron stood quite near —

DONNA ROSE.

And then you tore it down.
   [*Movement of terror on the part of* TORQUEMADA.

DON SANCHO.

        You 're right, it was
A first-rate lever. Thanks to that same cross,
The tomb was opened, you escaped alive.

TORQUEMADA (*aside*).

O heavens! they are damned!

DON SANCHO.

        We both worked hard:
I lifted up the stone, she threw her weight
Upon the bar, and so the pit was opened.

TORQUEMADA (*aside*).

A cross torn down! a major sacrilege!
The gulf, the eternal gulf, yawns under them!
They are beyond salvation. O great God!
Beyond the enormous shadow Calvary casts.
Oh, wretched ones! it is not with the King
They have to deal, it is with God.
[*To* DON SANCHO *and* DONNA ROSE.] Reflect.
Are you quite sure this lever was a cross?

DON SANCHO.

I am quite sure. 'T was standing at the foot
Of an old wall, deep in the withered grass.
I seized it with both hands.

TORQUEMADA (*aside*).

      A cross torn down!
A cross! No matter. I must save them; but
In different mode.
    [*He waves them an adieu with his hand.*
    I shall be with you soon.

DON SANCHO.

Here, in this gloomy hour, we have no friends,
No refuge; our salvation lies in you,
My lord.

TORQUEMADA.

   Oh, yes! I 'll surely save you both.
[*He goes out by the back, and is seen slowly descending the staircase.*

SCENE V.

Don Sancho, Donna Rose.

DONNA ROSE.

Let us upon our knees give thanks to God, —
Help from on high! The miracles that he
Hath wrought for us! How quick we are to hope!
Is it not true, Don Sancho? How we catch
At every branch! The man we saved is in
That house, and saves us too. Yes, I have faith,
I hope. Dost think I 'm right?

DON SANCHO.

         Yes, hope, my angel!
He owes to us his life, he gives us life.
Hope! Ah! my soul is drunk with rapturous joy!
      [*He draws her towards him.*
Come! come! let's breathe at last! This shadow made
By wings of seraphim, — it cools our brows
After so many woes. A hand is opened
Between us and the stars.

DONNA ROSE.

        Yes, 't is the hand
Of God who shields us.

DON SANCHO.

       Say, dost hear the songs
Of Paradise draw near?
    [*Pointing to the park and the clumps of trees.*
       All nature's like
The music of a lyre.

DONNA ROSE.

    Ah! now we see
Each other once again, what we would say
Starts to the lips, — the past, the present, all
We suffered, wished, or thought, the sleepless nights,
God and his mercy, men who are so wicked —
At last the soul flows over, and we say:
"I love thee!" then we know all has been said.
O love, I have wept much! When hope was lost,
When I have seen myself dragged to the cloister,
When I have seen the thread of our own fate
Dissevered, and our two hearts torn asunder,
And — oh! the horror of it — when I had
Some vague conception of the King's designs,
I felt myself tender at once and strong,

Invincible and proud, and, oh! how oft
I wished to die!
[*A dim moonlight is beginning to mingle with the dark
  perspective of the horizon.*

DON SANCHO.

                And I — But, Rose, let us
Forget it all. It is the heart alone
That lives, 't is love alone that stands. All else
Sinks down and dies. We are about to be —
Yes! married, saved! I place faith in this priest.
He gives us back what he received from us.
Ah, let us love and live! Behold the moon
Rise o'er yon mountains; see these waters, groves
Filled with an infinite soul. This beauty, Rose,
Means mercy. All the charms strewed round
This lovely spot bid us believe, and speak
Of God to us. Fear nothing, lovely soul!
O sinless soul, at peace at last! Grief is
The lily; hope, — it is the dew. When grief
Unfolds its leaves, God weeps from tenderness,
And that is hope. Our sorrows, cries, have moved him.
Guardians unawares preserve us. I
See shadows all around to do us service.
What should I say to thee? I love thee. Ah!
We're conquerors, and all the azure depths
Of heaven are in our hearts. Then let us hope!

DONNA ROSE.

Oh, yes! I feel some one shall set us free.
I hope. Hope is new birth.

DON SANCHO.
                      And love is life.

DONNA ROSE.

What had I in my mind? Ah! now I know!
I fain would say: I love thee!

DON SANCHO.
                    Then draw nigh.
                        [*She approaches him.*
Quite close.
[*She draws near to him. Both sink down on the bench,*
    DONNA ROSE *in the arms of* DON SANCHO.

DONNA ROSE (*gazing on him with absorbing earnestness*).
            Don Sancho! O my King! How fair
And radiant is thy face!

DON SANCHO.
                    We shall belong,
My Rose, to one another and forever!
How true it is, dear Rose! God comes whene'er
We pray to him. Dost thou discern the sense
Those heavenly words "wife, husband," bear? — Grace
    beauty,
And purity, thy sacred body and
Thy hallowed flesh — Oh, the hot sleepless nights,
The dreams within the cloister! — Oh, to be
The spouse! to seize the bashful, shrinking angel!
To see thee every moment, speak with thee
By night or day the words that tell our bliss,
And hear thee say them to me, tremulous,
And kiss them on thy smiling lips! and then —
Oh, do not blush! — my Rose, to see some day
Thy lovely charming bosom pressed between
The little adorable hands of a sweet babe,
Who is thy master while I am thy lover!
To hear him stammer with his honeyed lips:
"Mother!"

DONNA ROSE (*with an expression of adoration*).

And "Father!"— O my love!

[*During their ecstasy the top of a black banner appears behind the staircase. The banner mounts the staircase slowly. Then it is seen entire. It bears in the centre a death's head and two bones forming a cross, white on a black ground.* DON SANCHO *and* DONNA ROSE *turn round, and are struck dumb with terror. The banner continues to mount. Finally the cowl of the bannerbearer is perceived, and, on the right and left, the cowls of two files of white and black penitents appear.*

SANCHO.

O God!

THE END.

ESMERALDA

DRAMATIS PERSONÆ

Esmeralda.
Phœbus de Chateaupers.
Claude Frollo.
Quasimodo
Fleur-de-Lys.
Madame Aloise de Gondelaurier.
Diana.
Berangère.
Viscount de Gif.
M. de Chevreuse.
M. de Morlaix.
Clopin Frouillefou.
The Town-crier.

Populace, Vagrants, Archers, etc

ESMERALDA.

ACT I.

SCENE. — *The Court of Miracles. It is night. A crowd of vagrants. Noisy dancing. Male and female beggars in different attitudes of their profession. The King of Thune on his cask. Fires, lights, torches. In the shadow a circle of wretched dwellings.*

SCENE I.

CLAUDE FROLLO, CLOPIN FROUILLEFOU, *then* ESMERALDA, *then* QUASIMODO. THE VAGRANTS.

CHORUS OF VAGRANTS.

Long live Clopin! Long live the King of Thune!
Long live the rogues of Paris.
Let us strike our blows at dusk, —
The hour when all the cats are drunk.
Let us dance! Defy Pope and bull,
And let us laugh in our skins,
Whether April wets or June burns
The feathers in our caps.
Let us smell from afar
The shot of the avenging archer,
Or the bag of money which passes
On the back of the traveller.
In the light of the moon,
We will go dance with the spirits.
Long live Clopin, King of Thune!
Long live the rogues of Paris!

CLAUDE FROLLO (*apart behind a pillar in a corner of the stage. He is covered with a long cloak which hides his priestly garb*).

In the midst of this infamous band
What matters the sigh of a soul?
I suffer! Oh, never did fiercer flame
Burn in the bowels of a volcano.

[ESMERALDA *enters, dancing.*

CHORUS.

There she is! There she is! It is she — Esmeralda!

CLAUDE FROLLO (*aside*).

It is she! oh, yes — 't is she!
Wherefore, relentless fate,
Made you her so beautiful,
Me — so unfortunate?

[*She reaches the centre of the stage.* THE VAGRANTS *form an admiring circle around her.*

ESMERALDA.

An orphan am I,
　Child of woe,
To you I turn
　And flowers throw!
In my wild joy
　Sad sighs abide;
I show a smile,
　The tears I hide.

Poor girl, — I dance
　Where brooklets run,
As chirp the birds
　My song flows on:

I am the dove
  Which, hurt, must fall;
Over my cradle
  Hangs death's pall.

CHORUS.

Young girl, dance on!
  More gentle you make us.
Take us for family,
  And play with us,
As stoops the nightingale
  Unto the sea,
Teasing its waves
  To ecstasy.

'T is the young girl, —
  Child of woe,
When beams her eye
  Grief must go.
She 's like the bee
  Which trembling flies
To the flower's heart,
  Its Paradise.

Young girl, dance on!
  More gentle you make us.
Take us for family,
  And play with us!

CLAUDE FROLLO (*aside*).

Tremble, young girl, —
  The priest is jealous.

[CLAUDE *attempts to draw near to* ESMERALDA; *she turns away from him with a kind of horror. The procession of the Pope of Fools enters. Torches, lanterns, and music. In the middle of the procession, upon a litter surrounded with candles,* QUASIMODO, *decked with cope and mitre, is carried.*

CHORUS.

Salute him, clerks of Vasoche!
Shell-heaps, lubbers, beggars!
Salute him, all of you! He comes.
Behold the Pope of Fools!

CLAUDE FROLLO (*perceiving* QUASIMODO, *and starting toward him with a gesture of anger*).

Quasimodo! What a strange part to play!
Profanation! Here — Quasimodo!

QUASIMODO.

Great God! what do I hear?

CLAUDE FROLLO.

Come here, I tell you.

QUASIMODO (*jumping from the litter*).

Here I am!

CLAUDE FROLLO.

Be anathematized!

QUASIMODO.

God! it is himself!

CLAUDE FROLLO.

Outrageous audacity!

QUASIMODO.

Moment of terror.

CLAUDE FROLLO.

To your knees, traitor!

QUASIMODO.

Pardon me. Master!

CLAUDE FROLLO.

No! I am a priest.
[CLAUDE FROLLO *tears off* QUASIMODO'S *pontifical ornaments, and crushes them underfoot.* THE VAGRANTS *begin to murmur; they form menacing groups around him; he looks at them angrily.*

THE VAGRANTS.

He threatens us,
O comrades!
Here in this place,
Where we reign.

QUASIMODO.

What means the audacity
Of these robbers?
They menace him,
But we shall see!

CLAUDE FROLLO.

Race unclean,
You menace me.
Robbers — Jews —
But we shall see!
[*The anger of* THE VAGRANTS *bursts forth.*

THE VAGRANTS.

Stop! stop! stop!
Down with the mar-joy!
He shall pay for it with his head;
In vain he defends himself.

QUASIMODO.

Have respect for his head.
Let every one cease,

Or I change this festival
To a bloody battle.

CLAUDE FROLLO.

It is not about his head
That Frollo is troubled. [*Puts his hand on his heart.*
There is the tempest,
There is the battle!

[*At the moment when* THE VAGRANTS' *fury has reached its highest pitch,* CLOPIN FROUILLEFOU *appears at the back of the stage.*

CLOPIN.

Who in this infamous den
Dares to attack my lord the Archdeacon,
And Quasimodo, bell-ringer
Of Notre Dame?

THE VAGRANTS (*subsiding*).

It is Clopin, our King!

CLOPIN.

Clowns! Be off!

THE VAGRANTS.

We must obey!

CLOPIN.

Leave us!

[THE VAGRANTS *retire to their hovels. The Court of Miracles appears deserted.* CLOPIN *approaches* CLAUDE *cautiously.*

SCENE II.

CLAUDE FROLLO, QUASIMODO, CLOPIN FROUILLEFOU.

CLOPIN.

What purpose brings you to this orgy?
Has your lordship any orders to give me?
You are my master in sorcery;
Speak, — I will do all.

CLAUDE FROLLO (*grasping* CLOPIN'S *arm excitedly, and dragging him to the front of the stage*).

I have come to end all.
Listen!

CLOPIN.

My lord!

CLAUDE FROLLO.

I love her more than ever.
You behold me quivering with love and with anguish.
I must have her to-night.

CLOPIN.

You will see her pass by here, — in a moment;
It is the way to her home.

CLAUDE FROLLO (*aside*).

Oh! Hell has hold of me!
[*Aloud.*] Soon — you say?

CLOPIN.

Upon the instan

CLAUDE FROLLO.

Alone?

CLOPIN.

Alone.

CLAUDE FROLLO.

That is enough.

CLOPIN.

Will you wait?

CLAUDE FROLLO.

I wait, —
Let me have her, or let me die!

CLOPIN.

Can I help you?

CLAUDE FROLLO.

No!
[*He motions to* CLOPIN *to leave him, after having thrown him his purse. When he finds himself alone with* QUASIMODO, *he draws him to the front of the stage.*

CLAUDE FROLLO.

Come! I need you!

QUASIMODO.

It is well!

CLAUDE FROLLO.

For a deed that is impious, frightful, awful!

QUASIMODO.

You are my lord and master!

CLAUDE FROLLO.

Chains, death, the law, —
We brave them all.

QUASIMODO.
Count upon me.

CLAUDE FROLLO (*recklessly*).
I mean to abduct the gypsy!

QUASIMODO.
Master, take my blood — without telling me why!
[*Upon a sign from* CLAUDE FROLLO *he retires up stage and leaves his master down stage.*

CLAUDE FROLLO.
Oh, Heaven! to have given one's mind to the depths,
To have tried all the crimes of sorcery,
To have fallen lower than hell itself:
A priest, at midnight, in the dark to watch for a woman!
And to reflect that in this state in which I find my soul
  God sees me!

      Well! what does it matter?
        Fate drags me on!
      Its hand is too strong,
        Its will be done!
      I begin life over, —
        The priest insane
      Feels hope no longer,
        Knows terror is vain!
      Demon, who drugs me,
        Give her to me;
      And I, who evoked thee,
        Thy slave will be, —
      Receive the priest
        Whose bonds are riven!
      Hell with her
        Will be my heaven!

Come, exquisite woman,
   Your beauty I claim.
You shall own me forever,
   I swear, in God's name!
Since he — since the master
   By whom love was given,
Bids me choose, — me, a priest,
   Between passion and heaven!

QUASIMODO (*returning*).

Master, the moment is at hand!

CLAUDE FROLLO.

                     Yes — the solemn hour
It will decide my fate. Be silent! Hush!

CLAUDE FROLLO *and* QUASIMODO.

The night is dark,
   Footsteps I hear:
In shadow does not
   Some one draw near?
   [*They go to the back of the stage to listen.*

THE WATCH (*passing behind the houses*).

Vigilance and peace!
   Whoever passes here
Must ope the eye to darkness,
   To silence strain the ear.

CLAUDE FROLLO *and* QUASIMODO.

In shadow they come;
   They make no sound:
Still let us be
   While the watch goes round!
   [*The voices of the watch grow fainter.*

QUASIMODO.

The watch has passed!

CLAUDE FROLLO.

Our terror follows it.

[CLAUDE FROLLO *and* QUASIMODO *look anxiously at the door through which* ESMERALDA *must pass.*

QUASIMODO.

Love inspires,
  Hope renders strong,
Him who watches
  While sleeps the throng.
I see her come, —
  Lo! she appears.
Maid divine!
  Have no fears!

CLAUDE FROLLO.

Love inspires,
  Hope renders strong,
Him who watches
  While sleeps the throng.
I see her come,
  Maid divine!
Lo! she appears, —
  She is mine!

[ESMERALDA *enters: they throw themselves upon her and try to drag her away: she struggles.*

ESMERALDA.

Help, — help! To me, — help!

CLAUDE FROLLO *and* QUASIMODO.

Hush, young maiden, — hush!

SCENE III.

ESMERALDA, QUASIMODO, PHŒBUS DE CHATEAUPERS, *the archers of the watch.*

PHŒBUS (*entering at the head of a body of archers*).
In the King's name!
[*In the struggle* CLAUDE *escapes. The archers seize* QUASIMODO.

PHŒBUS.

Arrest him! hold him close!
Be he lord or valet!
At once — we will conduct him
To the prison Chatelet.
[*The archers take* QUASIMODO *up stage and off.* ESMERALDA, *recovered from her fright, approaches* PHŒBUS *with curiosity, mingled with admiration, and draws him gently to the front of the stage.*

ESMERALDA (*to* PHŒBUS).

Deign to tell me
Your name, sir!
I beg you to.

PHŒBUS.

Phœbus, my child, —
Of the family
Of Chateaupers.

ESMERALDA.

Captain?

PHŒBUS.

Yes, my queen!

ESMERALDA.

Queen? oh, no!

PHŒBUS.

Exquisite grace!

ESMERALDA.

Phœbus! I like your name!

PHŒBUS.

Upon my soul
I have a blade
Which has, Madame,
   Great havoc made.

ESMERALDA (*to* PHŒBUS).

A beautiful captain,
   An officer grand,
With corselet of steel
   And an air of command!
Often, kind sir,
   Our hearts they break,
And only laugh
   At the tears they make.

PHŒBUS (*aside*).

With a beautiful captain,
   An officer gay,
Love hardly succeeds
   In living a day.
All soldiers desire
   To pluck every rose,
Joys without troubles,
   Love without woes.

PHŒBUS (*to* ESMERALDA).

A radiant spirit
Smiles at me
Through thine eyes.

ESMERALDA.

A beautiful captain,
　An officer grand,
With corselet of steel
　And an air of command!
Long watches the girl
　He carelessly passed;
And the dreams he awakened
　Forever may last!

PHŒBUS.

With a beautiful captain,
　An officer gay,
Love hardly succeeds
　In living a day!
It's like lightning which flashes, —
　This eager desire
Which the eyes of sweet maidens
　Kindle to fire!

ESMERALDA (*standing before the* CAPTAIN *and admiring him*).

My lord Phœbus! Let me see you!
Let me admire you a hundred fold!
Oh the beautiful scarf of silk, —
Oh the fine scarf with fringe of gold!

　　　　　[PHŒBUS *takes it off and offers it to her*

PHŒBUS.

Does it please you?

ESMERALDA (*taking the scarf and putting it on*).

Yes, it is beautiful!

PHŒBUS.

One moment! [*He goes to her and tries to embrace her*

ESMERALDA (*drawing back*).

Don't, I beg you!

PHŒBUS (*insisting*).

You must kiss me!

ESMERALDA (*drawing away still more*)

No, truly!

PHŒBUS (*laughing*).
A beauty
So cruel,
So haughty,
Is charming.

ESMERALDA.

No, beautiful captain,
In vain you plead!
Can I tell how far
A kiss might lead?

PHŒBUS.

I am a captain,
Why abuse me?
I want a kiss, —
Don't refuse me!
Give it me, — give it, or I will take!

ESMERALDA.

No, leave me! I beg of you, for my sake.

PHŒBUS.

One kiss, one kiss, — 't is nothing, you see.

ESMERALDA.

Nothing to you, but much to me!

PHŒBUS.

Look at me, dear! I am playing no part!

ESMERALDA.

Alas, but I cannot look into my heart!

PHŒBUS.

To-night love shall make an entrance there!

ESMERALDA.

Wherever love enters, soon follows despair.
[*She slips out of his arms and escapes.* PHŒBUS, *disappointed, turns to* QUASIMODO, *whom the archers hold bound at the back of the stage.*

PHŒBUS.

She escapes me, she resists me!
A gay adventure, verily!
I keep the worst of our two birds of prey, —
The owl remains; the nightingale flew away!
[*He places himself at the head of his guard and goes out, taking* QUASIMODO *with him.*

CHORUS OF THE WATCH.

Vigilance and peace, —
Whoever passes here
Must ope the eye to darkness,
To silence strain the ear!
[*The sound grows fainter and finally ceases.*

ACT II.

SCENE. — *The square of Grève. The pillory.* QUASIMODO *is in the pillory. Populace on the square.*

SCENE I.

CHORUS.

He abducted a girl, —
What! is it possible?
Hark! how they abuse him!
Do you hear, my friends?
Quasimodo has been hunting on Cupid's domain!

A WOMAN OF THE PEOPLE.

He will pass through my street
On his return from the pillory;
And it is Pierrat Forterne
Who will give us the signal.

TOWN-CRIER.

In the King's name, whom God protect!
The man you see here, will be put
Under a strong guard,
In the pillory for one hour.

CHORUS.

Down with him! Down with him!
The hunchback, the deaf, the one-eyed creature
        This Barabbas!
I believe, s'death! he's looking at us.
Down with the sorcerer!
He makes faces. he kicks:

He makes dogs bark in the streets.
Punish the rascal well!
Double the whip and the penalty.

QUASIMODO.

Drink!

CHORUS.

Hang him!

QUASIMODO.

Drink!

CHORUS.

Be accursed!

[ESMERALDA, *some instants ago, joined the crowd. She perceives* QUASIMODO, *first with surprise, then with pity. Suddenly, in the midst of all the noise, she mounts the pillory, unfastens a little cup which she carries on her belt, and gives a drink to* QUASIMODO.

CHORUS.

What are you doing, beautiful girl?
Leave Quasimodo alone!
When Beelzebub roasts,
Nobody gives him water.

[*She comes down. The archers unfasten* QUASIMODO *and take him away.*

CHORUS.

He abducted a woman!
Who? This dolt!
It is terrible, it is infamous,
It is too much!
Do you hear, my friends?
Quasimodo
Dared to go hunting on Cupid's domain.

SCENE II.

A magnificent drawing-room in which people are making preparations for a festival. PHŒBUS, FLEUR-DE-LYS, MADAME ALOISE DE GONDELAURIEE.

MADAME ALOISE.

Phœbus, my future son-in-law, listen to me. I am fond of you.
Be master here, as if you were another self.
Look to it that every one is gay to-night.
And you, my daughter, come, get ready.
You will be the most beautiful at this festival,
Be also the most happy.
[*She goes up stage and gives orders to the servants, who continue the preparations.*

FLEUR-DE-LYS.

Sir, since the other week,
We have hardly seen you twice!
This festival brings you back.
How fortunate for us!

PHŒBUS.

Don't scold, I beg of you!

FLEUR-DE-LYS.

I understand. Phœbus forgets me!

PHŒBUS.

I swear to you —

FLEUR-DE-LYS.

Don't swear!
They only swear who deceive.

PHŒBUS.

Forget you? What folly!
Are you not the most fair?
Am I not the most loving?

PHŒBUS (*aside*).

My beautiful betrothed
 Is out of sorts to-day;
Suspicion is in her mind.
 What a pity!
Beauties, the lovers you treat ill
 Go elsewhere.
You can do more with pleasure
 Than with tears.

FLEUR-DE-LYS (*aside*).

To betray me, his betrothed,
 Who belong to him!
I, who have only him to think of
 And worry about!
Ah! whether he is away or here,
 What grief!
Present, he scorns my joy;
 Absent, my tears.

FLEUR-DE-LYS.

Phœbus, the scarf that I worked for you,—
What have you done with it? I don't see it

PHŒBUS (*troubled*).

The scarf? I don't know!
[*Aside.*] Good God! unlucky chance!

FLEUR-DE-LYS.

You forgot it?
 [*Aside.*] To whom has he given it?
And for whom am I deserted?

MADAME ALOISE (*coming up to them and trying to reconcile them*).

Heavens! get married! Then you can quarrel.

PHŒBUS (*to* FLEUR-DE-LYS).

No! I have not forgotten it.
I remember, I carefully folded it
And put it in an enamelled box
That I had made for it.
[*Passionately to* FLEUR-DE-LYS, *who still frets.*
I swear I love you better
Than one could love Venus herself!

FLEUR-DE-LYS.

Don't swear! Don't swear!
They only swear who deceive!

MADAME ALOISE.

Children, don't quarrel, — everything is bright to-day!
Come, my daughter, you must be seen!
The guests are coming! Everything has its turn.
[*To the servants.*] Light the candles and let the ball begin.
I want everything to be beautiful, to seem as bright as day.

PHŒBUS.

Since we have Fleur-de-lys, nothing is wanting to the ball.

FLEUR-DE-LYS.

Yes, Phœbus, — love is wanting! [*They go out.*

PHŒBUS (*watching* FLEUR-DE-LYS *go out*).

She speaks the truth: my heart is sad
   Even when she is near —
The one I love, the one who fills my soul, —
   Alas! she is not here.

Exquisite creature,
　　To you my love!
Oh, dancing shadow,
　　My sweet-voiced dove,
Absent, yet with me
　　Wherever I move!

She's as bewildering and sweet
　　As is a nest mid rushes,
Sweet as a rosebud crowned with moss,
　　Sweet as the joy which sorrow hushes.

Humble child and virgin proud,
　　Soul that's pure though free!
Voluptuous ardours sink abashed
　　Before thy chastity.

In the dark night she comes,
　　An angel from the skies;
Her forehead veiled by shadows,
　　Flames darting from her eyes.

I see her face forever, —
　　Now bright, now dark it seems;
But strangely — 't is in heaven
　　I see her in these dreams.

　　Exquisite creature,
　　　　To you my love!
　　Oh, dancing shadow,
　　　　My sweet-voiced dove,
　　Absent, yet with me
　　　　Wherever I move!
　　　　[*Enter several lords and ladies in gala dress*

SCENE III.

The preceding. VISCOUNT DE GIF, M. DE MORLAIX, M. DE CHEVREUSE, MADAME DE GONDELAURIER, FLEUR-DE-LYS, DIANA, BÉRANGÈRE. *Ladies, Lords.*

VISCOUNT DE GIF.
My salutations, noble hostesses!

MADAME ALOISE, PHŒBUS, FLEUR-DE-LYS *(bowing,*
Good evening, noble viscount!
Forget all care and grief
Beneath this hospitable roof.

M. DE MORLAIX.
Ladies, may God send you
Health, pleasure, and happiness!

MADAME ALOISE, PHŒBUS, FLEUR-DE-LYS.
May Heaven return with interest
All your good wishes, my lord!

M. DE CHEVREUSE.
Ladies, from the bottom of my soul
I belong to you, as I do to God!

MADAME ALOISE, PHŒBUS, FLEUR-DE-LYS.
Kind sir, may our good Lady
Come always to your aid!

[*All the guests enter.*

CHORUS.
Come to the festival, come!
Page, lordship, and ladyship, come!

With flowers in your hand,
A joy-seeking band,
Come to the festival, come!

[*The guests greet and salute each other; servants circulate among the crowd, bearing platters laden with flowers and fruits. A group of young girls forms itself near a window to the left. Suddenly one of them calls to the others, and motions to them to look out of the window.*

DIANA (*looking out*).

Come and look! come and look, Bérangère!

BÉRANGÈRE (*looking into the street*).

Is n't she quick? Is n't she light?

DIANA.

It is a fairy or it is love.

VISCOUNT DE GIF (*laughing*).

Who dances in the public square?

M. DE CHEVREUSE (*after having looked*).

Indeed! it is the magician.
Phœbus, it is your gypsy
Whom, the other night, with valor
You saved from a robber.

VISCOUNT DE GIF.

Oh, yes. it is the gypsy.

M. DE MORLAIX.

She's as beautiful as the day.

DIANA (*to* PHŒBUS).

If you know her tell her to come
And dance for us.

PHŒBUS (*looking out with an absent air*).

It might be she!
[*To* M. DE GIF.] Do you think she would remember?

FLEUR-DE-LYS (*who watches and listens*).

Every one remembers you.
Come, call her, tell her to come up.
[*Aside.*] I will see whether to believe what I am told.

PHŒBUS (*to* FLEUR-DE-LYS).

You wish it? Well, let us try!
[*He motions to the dancer to come up.*

THE YOUNG GIRLS.

She is coming!

M. DE CHEVREUSE.

She has disappeared under the porch.

DIANA.

She has left the mob, stupefied.

VISCOUNT DE GIF.

Ladies, you will see the nymph of the streets.

FLEUR-DE-LYS (*aside*).

How quickly she obeyed that sign from Phœbus!

SCENE IV.

The same. ESMERALDA. *The gypsy enters timidly, confused and radiant. Movement of admiration. The crowd falls back before her.*

CHORUS.

Look! her brow is fair amid the fairest,
As a star would shine, surrounded by torches.

PHŒBUS.

   Oh, creature divine!
      Admiration is duty.
   Of this ball she is queen,
      Her crown is her beauty.
[*He turns to* MESSIEURS DE GIF *and* DE CHEVREUSE.
   Friends, my soul is on fire.
      War and death would I face,
   To hold in my arms
      Such bewildering grace.

M. DE CHEVREUSE.

   She is a heavenly vision,
      A dream most rare and tender,
   Which, floating through earth's darkness,
      Radiates celestial splendor.
   Born in the public streets, —
      Oh, blind caprice of fate,
   To trail through muddy streams
      A flower so immaculate!

ESMERALDA (*fixing her eyes on* PHŒBUS *in the crowd*).
   It is my Phœbus, I was sure,
      Just as that night I found him;

Whether in satin or in steel,
  How grace and strength surround him!
Phœbus, — my head is all on fire,
  All burns within me, joy and pain;
My soul's consumed for lack of tears,
  Just as earth yearns for rain.

FLEUR-DE-LYS.

How fair she is, — yes, I was sure!
  Jealous, indeed, I ought to be;
But yet to match that loveliness
  How great must be my jealousy!
Alas! perhaps we both, foredoomed
  To waste 'neath sorrow's harsh caress,
Full soon shall die, — she in her flower,
  I in my loneliness!

MADAME ALOISE.

A radiant creature, truly,
  But, faith, 't is a disgrace
That such a wretched gypsy
  Should have so sweet a face.
Alas! the curious laws of fate
  'T is not for mortal mind to know:
The serpent hides his treacherous head
  Beneath the fairest flowers that grow.

ALL (*together*).

She has the calmness, the delight
Of radiant skies on a warm night.

MADAME ALOISE (*to* ESMERALDA).

Come, child! My beauty, come, —
Come and dance us some new dance!
[ESMERALDA *prepares to dance, and draws from her bosom
  the scarf which* PHŒBUS *gave her.*

FLEUR-DE-LYS.

My scarf! Phœbus, you have deceived me!
My rival! Here she is!
[FLEUR-DE-LYS *snatches the scarf from* ESMERALDA, *and
falls in a swoon. All the people rush angrily toward
the gypsy, who flies for protection to* PHŒBUS.

ALL.

Is it true that Phœbus loves her?
   Infamous creature, go — depart!
To brave us thus in our own home,
   You must have an audacious heart.
Oh! height of insolence! Retire!
   Go back into the public street!
The common tradesmen, they can praise
   The jumping of your low-born feet.
Away with her, away at once!
   Out at the door! 'T is a disgrace
For this degraded girl to lift
   Her eyes to such a lofty place.

ESMERALDA.

Oh, defend me! Help! Defend me,
   Save me, Phœbus, I implore thee;
For the poor forsaken gypsy,
   Stands defenceless now before thee!

PHŒBUS.

I love her, and I love but her.
   Yes! her defender I will be.
I 'll fight for her, and my strong arm
   Will bear my heart out valiantly.
If some one must be her protector,
   I am the one, — and doubt me not,
Her wrongs are mine, and who insults her
   Must answer for it on the spot.

ALL.

What! She is what he loves! Indeed!
Away from here, away from here!
A gypsy he prefers to us;
With loving words he calms her fear.
Hush! silence! Both of you be still!
No further words of insolence.
[*To* PHŒBUS.] From you, 't is too much arrogance!
[*To* ESMERALDA.] From thee, too much impertinence!
[PHŒBUS *and his friends protect the gypsy, who is menaced by all the guests of* MADAME DE GONDELAURIER. ESMERALDA *staggers toward the door.*

ACT III.

SCENE. — *The front yard of a tavern. Tavern to the right; trees to the left. In the back a door, and a small low wall which closes in the yard. In the distance the roof of Notre Dame with its towers and its spire. A dark silhouette of old Paris outlines itself against the red sunset. The river Seine is at the base of the picture.*

SCENE I.

PHŒBUS, VISCOUNT DE GIF, M. DE MORLAIX, M. DE CHEVREUSE, *and many other friends of* PHŒBUS, *seated at tables, are drinking, and singing; afterward* DON CLAUDE FROLLO.

CHORUS.

Be propitious and well-inclined,
  Our Lady of Saint Lo,
To him who only water hates
  Of all things here below!

PHŒBUS.

Give to the brave
  In every place
A well-filled cellar,
  A pretty face.
Happy fellow!
  Help him hold
Dainty women,
  Wine that's old.

If a beauty
  Of cold mien
Be unwilling,
  'T is sometimes seen.

He jokes with her
   With merry winks,
Then he sings,
   Then he drinks!

The day goes by.
   Or drunk or not,
He soon embraces
   His Toinotte;
Then ferocious
   He goes to bed
In a cannon's mouth,
   And sleeps like lead!

And his soul,
   Which often seems
To mix up women
   With his dreams,
Is contented if the wind,
   With its come and go,
Rocks the canvas of his tent
   Gently to and fro!

CHORUS.

Be propitious and well inclined,
   Our Lady of Saint Lo!
To him who only water hates
   Of all things here below.

[*Enter* CLAUDE FROLLO, *who seats himself at a table at some distance from* PHŒBUS, *and appears at first to observe nothing that passes around him.*

VISCOUNT DE GIF (*to* PHŒBUS).

That pretty gypsy,
What are you doing with her?
   [CLAUDE FROLLO *makes a movement of attention.*

PHŒBUS.

To-night, in an hour,
I have a meeting with her.

ALL.

Truly?

PHŒBUS.

Truly!
[*The agitation of* CLAUDE FROLLO *increases.*

VISCOUNT DE GIF.

In one hour?

PHŒBUS.

In one moment!
Oh, love! supremest rapture!
To feel one heart holds two!
To own the woman that one loves, —
Be slave and conqueror too!
To have her soul; to have her charms,
Her song which fills with bliss;
To see her sweet eyes wet with tears,
To dry them with a kiss.
[*While he sings, the others drink and strike their glasses.*

CHORUS.

'T is a rapture supreme,
Whatever one thinks,
To drink to one's love,
And to love what one drinks!

PHŒBUS.

Friends, the prettiest of all,
A grace divine,
Oh, wonder, ecstasy!
Friends, she is mine!

CLAUDE FROLLO (*aside*).

I bind myself to hell;
Misfortune on you dwell!

PHŒBUS.

Pleasure awaits us;
  Exhaust without remorse
The better part of life,
  Love's precious intercourse!
What matter if one dies,
  When joy has passed away,
I'd give a century for an hour,
  Eternity for a day.

[*The curfew rings; the friends of* PHŒBUS *arise from the table, replace their swords, their caps, their cloaks, and prepare to depart.*

CHORUS.

Phœbus, the hour is come;
  It is the curfew-bell:
Hurry to your beloved;
  God's blessing on you dwell!

PHŒBUS.

At last the hour is come;
  It is the curfew-bell.
I go to my beloved;
  God's blessing on her dwell!

[*The friends of* PHŒBUS *go out.*

SCENE II.

CLAUDE FROLLO, PHŒBUS. CLAUDE FROLLO *stops* PHŒBUS *as he is about to go out.*

CLAUDE FROLLO.

Captain!

PHŒBUS.
Who is this man?

CLAUDE FROLLO.
Listen to me!

PHŒBUS.
Make haste!

CLAUDE FROLLO.

Do you know the name of the one
Who awaits you at the meeting to-night?

PHŒBUS.

By my life, it is my beauty!
The one I love and who loves me.
My song-bird, my dancing gypsy,
My Esmeralda, it is she!

CLAUDE FROLLO.
It is death!

PHŒBUS.
Friend! First, you are an idiot;
Second, go to the devil!

CLAUDE FROLLO.
Listen!

PHŒBUS.
What do I care?

CLAUDE FROLLO.

Phœbus, if you cross the threshold of that door —

PHŒBUS.

You are mad!

CLAUDE FROLLO.

You are dead!
Tremble! One of the gypsies she!
No law protects those awful places.
There love's a masquerade for hate,
  Death lies concealed in their embraces.

PHŒBUS (*laughing*).

My dear sir, readjust your cape,
  Return unto your fools' retreat!
Strange they allow you to escape!
May Esculapius, Jupiter, the Devil,
  Thither conduct your straying feet!

CLAUDE FROLLO.

Truly they are faithless women;
  Believe that the report speaks true.
Darkness strange and deep surrounds them;
  Phœbus! there death waits for you!

[CLAUDE FROLLO'S *earnestness seems to trouble* PHŒBUS, *who looks at his interrogator with anxiety.*

PHŒBUS.

He astounds me!
Ah, he wounds me
In spite of myself, with doubt!
This city great
Is full of hate,
And treachery is all about!

CLAUDE FROLLO.

 I astound him,
 And I wound him,
In spite of himself, with doubt.
 The fool, he fears,
 And sees and hears
Nothing but treachery about.

Believe me, — my lord, avoid the siren
Who lures you to destruction.
More than one gypsy in her rage
Has stabbed a heart palpitating with love.
[PHŒBUS, *whom he tries to drag along, recovers himself and pushes him off.*

PHŒBUS.

 Have I become a fool?
 Gypsy, Jewess, or Moor,
The love that questions what she be
 Is love most base and poor.
 The fateful hour is come,
  Unto my love I fly!
 If death be but as sweet as she,
  It will be fine to die!

CLAUDE FROLLO (*holding him*).

Consider! A gypsy!
 Your folly is great.
How dare you thus rashly
 Trifle with fate!
Oh, dread the false creature
 Who waits in the gloom,
And do not thus wildly
 Rush to your doom.
[PHŒBUS *exits quickly, in spite of* CLAUDE FROLLO. CLAUDE FROLLO *stands gloomy and undecided for a noment; then follows* PHŒBUS.

SCENE III.

A chamber. In the background, a window which opens on the river. CLOPIN FROUILLEFOU *enters, bearing a torch. He is followed by several men, to whom he makes a preconcerted sign, and places them in a dark corner, in which they disappear; then he returns to the door and signals to some one to come up.* DON CLAUDE *appears.*

CLOPIN (*to* CLAUDE).

From here you can see the captain
And the gypsy without being seen.
      [*He shows him an alcove behind some tapestry.*

CLAUDE FROLLO.

The men are stationed and ready?

CLOPIN.

                    They are ready.

CLAUDE FROLLO.

The projector of this must never be known.
Silence! take this purse.
I will give you as much more afterwards.
[CLAUDE FROLLO *hides himself in the alcove.* CLOPIN *exits with caution.* ESMERALDA *and* PHŒBUS *enter.*

CLAUDE FROLLO (*aside*).

    Oh, woman adored,
      Destiny's prey!
    She enters in beauty,
      In tears goes away.

ESMERALDA (*to* PHŒBUS).
My lord the count,
 My feelings I try to hide.
My heart is filled with shame,
 And filled also with pride.

PHŒBUS (*to* ESMERALDA).
My beauty, white and red,
 I beg you blush no more.
Love, entering love's domain,
 Leaves fear outside the door.

[PHŒBUS *makes* ESMERALDA *sit down on the bench beside him.*

PHŒBUS.
Dost thou love me?

ESMERALDA.
I love thee!

CLAUDE FROLLO (*aside*).
What torture!

PHŒBUS.
The adorable creature!
Upon my soul, you are divine!

ESMERALDA.
Your lips are flatterers;
You make me feel ashamed.
I beg of you, don't come so near.

CLAUDE FROLLO.
They love each other. How I envy them!

ESMERALDA.
My Phœbus! I owe my life to you.

PHŒBUS.

And I — I owe my happiness to you.

PHŒBUS.

ESMERALDA.

Be good to me!
Oh, try to be
Gentle, I entreat,
To the young maid,
Who much afraid
Trembles at your feet!

PHŒBUS.

Oh, my white queen,
Goddess serene,
Sovereign of beauty,
Whose bright eyes shine
With fires divine
Of passion and of duty!

CLAUDE FROLLO.

I wait for them;
I hark to them.
How tender she,
How handsome he!
How near their doom!
Be joyous he,
And happy she,
While I prepare their tomb!

PHŒBUS.

Nymph or woman,
Saint or human,
Be my wife to me!
All day I yearn,
All night I burn,
Such is my love for thee!

ESMERALDA.

I am woman,
I am human,
And my soul afire,
Trembles ever,
Longs forever,
As throbs a lover's lyre!

CLAUDE FROLLO.

Woman, wait!
My flame as great,
My blade must have its turn.
Oh! I admire
These souls afire,
And these hearts which burn!

PHŒBUS.

Be always white and red, my love,
And smile at our bright lot;
Smile sweet at love, which we've awaked,
And chastity, which we've forgot.
Your mouth is heaven, — my heaven, love, —
My soul would cling in bliss
Upon it, love, and pray that life
Might end with one long kiss.

ESMERALDA.

Your voice delights my ear, love;
Your smile is sweet and free.
The laughing passion in your eyes
Benumbs and conquers me.
Your wishes are my law, love,
But I can't yield to this:
My virtue and my happiness
Might die in that long kiss!

CLAUDE FROLLO.

Don't let them hear your step, Death,
   As near to them you creep!
My jealous hatred will keep watch
   While their love falls asleep.
From out their arms so closely locked
   You'll steal away their bliss!
Phœbus — your wish is granted,
   You die for that long kiss!

[CLAUDE FROLLO *rushes upon* PHŒBUS *and stabs him; then he opens the window in the back, through which he escapes. With a great cry,* ESMERALDA *falls upon the body of* PHŒBUS. *The men stationed at the corner rush forward, seize her, and seem to accuse her.*

ACT IV.

SCENE. — *A prison. Door in the centre.*

SCENE I.

ESMERALDA (*alone, chained, lying upon a bed of straw*)
 What! He in the tomb and I in this cell, —
  He a victim and I a prisoner!
 I saw him fall! In truth, he's dead!
  And this crime, this awful crime, —
  They say it is my work!
 The stem of our life, while yet green, is broken.
 Phœbus has gone, and he shows me the way.
  Yesterday they made his grave,
  To-morrow they'll make mine!

ROMANCE.

Phœbus, is there nothing left,
No help given, to those bereft
 In this cruel wise, —
Neither filters, love, nor charms,
To assuage the soul's alarms,
 Or reopen closèd eyes?

God in heaven, I adore thee!
Every hour I implore thee!
Deign to end my life to-day
Or to take my love away!

Phœbus, let us turn our wings
 Toward the lights supernal,
Where all things must go at last,

Where love bides and is eternal.
On earth our bodies sleep together,
In heaven our souls will live forever!

God in heaven, I adore thee!
Every hour I implore thee!
Deign to end my life to-day
Or to take my love away!

[*The door opens.* CLAUDE FROLLO *enters, a lamp in his hand, his hood pulled over his face: he comes and stands, motionless, in front of* ESMERALDA.

ESMERALDA (*jumping up with terror*).

Who is this man?

CLAUDE FROLLO (*covered by his hood*).

A priest!

ESMERALDA.

A priest! How mysterious!

CLAUDE FROLLO.

Are you ready?

ESMERALDA.

Ready for what?

CLAUDE FROLLO.

Ready to die.

ESMERALDA.

Yes.

CLAUDE FROLLO.

It is well.

ESMERALDA.

Will it be soon? Answer me, father!

CLAUDE FROLLO.

Do you suffer so much?

ESMERALDA.
Yes, I suffer.

CLAUDE FROLLO.
Perhaps I, who shall live to-morrow,
Suffer more than you.

ESMERALDA.
You? Who, then, are you?

CLAUDE FROLLO.
The tomb lies between us!

ESMERALDA.
Your name?

CLAUDE FROLLO.
You wish to know it?

ESMERALDA.
Yes. [*He lifts his hood.*
The priest!
It is the priest! O God! my feeble strength inspire!
It is indeed his brow of ice, it is his glance of fire!
'T is he who has pursued me, remorseless, day and night;
'T was he who killed my Phœbus, and slew my heart's delight.
Monster, from my prison, with death's cold hand on me,
I'll curse thee, till within the grave my lips shall silent be!
What have I done to thee? What is thine awful plan?
What dost thou want with me, relentless, impious man?
You hate me!

CLAUDE FROLLO.
I love you!
I love you, — it is infamous!
Oh, shame to my priesthood!
This love, it is my soul;
This love, it is my blood!

At your feet I fall;
   Hear my heart, which cries,
   I prefer your tomb
   Unto Paradise.
Pity me. I love you! Your pity I implore!
For you I've sinned. Have mercy, do not curse me more

ESMERALDA.

He loves me! Oh, crown of horrors!
He holds me, — this horrible sorcerer!

CLAUDE FROLLO.

The only living thing in me
Is my love and my anguish!
   Hopeless anguish,
      Wretched plight!
   Alas! I love her
      Painful night!

ESMERALDA.

Awful moment,
   Cruel fright!
Heaven! He loves me,
   Fearful night!

CLAUDE FROLLO (*aside*).

She shudders, quivers in my arms;
   The priest has won his chance at last!
By night I bore her, once, away;
   Now, in the day, I'll hold her fast!
Death, which follows in my train,
Will give her back to love again!

ESMERALDA.

Pity, — pity, let me go!
Phœbus is dead: he waits above.

Alas! I tremble, I'm afraid,
I shiver at your frightful love,
E'en as the bird which, tortured, dies
Beneath the vulture's cruel eyes!

CLAUDE FROLLO.

Accept me, I love you! Refuse me no more!
Have pity for me, for yourself, I implore!

ESMERALDA.

Your prayer is an insult.

CLAUDE FROLLO.

Would you rather die?

ESMERALDA.

The body dies, — the soul lives!

CLAUDE FROLLO.

To die is terrible!

ESMERALDA.

Hush! your impious words!
Your love makes death beautiful!

CLAUDE FROLLO.

Choose! choose! Or Claude or death!
[CLAUDE *falls at* ESMERALDA'S *feet in supplication. She repels him.*

ESMERALDA.

No, murderer, I will not! Hush!
A crime is this foul love you've nursed.
Better the tomb to which I fly, —
Be cursed amid the most accursed!

CLAUDE FROLLO.
Tremble, for the scaffold claims you!
You know not what awful schemes
This breast of fury has engendered;
And hell abets me in my dreams.
How I love thee!
Thy hand give,
And to-morrow
Thou shalt live!
Night benumbed
With terror's breath!
Tears for me,
For thee death!
Say, "I love thee!"
Cease thy scorning;
Thy last day
Is dawning!
Ah! since in vain I supplicate,
In vain thy hate I fight,
Farewell forever! One day more,
Then comes eternal night.

ESMERALDA.
Inhuman priest,
Go! I abhor thee!
His dear blood yet
Seems dripping o'er thee!
Oh, night of horror,
Night of shame!
Enough of tears;
Death I claim!
In prison I brave thee,
In chains defy!
Be thou accursed
Eternally!

Thy passion be thy punishment!
To God my love leads me:
The gates of heaven he'll open,
But hell shall close o'er thee!

[*A jailer appears.* CLAUDE FROLLO *signs to him to lead out* ESMERALDA. *He exits while they drag forth the gypsy.*

SCENE II.

The area before Notre Dame; the front of the church. The sound of bells is heard.

QUASIMODO.

My God! I love,
Except myself,
All that's here, —
The air which passes,
And which chases
Away care;
And the swallow
Who is faithful
To the old roof;
The chapels high
O'ershadowed by
The Holy Cross;
Every rose
That grows;
Every sight
Of delight!

Sad creature, I, —
Uncouth, ill-made!

None envies me!
This is life
As it is!
Darkest night,
Bluest sky,
What matters it?
Every door
Leads to God.
Ignoble scabbard,
Noble blade;
Fair my soul
God has made.

Ring, bells small and great,—
Ring on, ring on!
Mix well your voices,
Gruff and sweet!
In the turrets,
In the tower,
Sing your song!

How they ring!
With all their might,
Let them hum
Day and night!
Our festival shall be
Magnificent, I swear!
Assail it fiercer yet,
The palpitating air!
The stupid peasants run,
And o'er the bridges tear!

Let them ring,
Let them hum,
Day and night!

Every feast
Is increased
By their might!
    [*He turns toward the front of the church.*
I saw black hangings in the chapel.
Are they dragging some misery here?
God! a presentiment! I'll not believe it!
[*Enter* CLAUDE FROLLO *and* CLOPIN *without perceiving* QUASIMODO.
It is my master! I'll observe him. He is gloomy too!
    [*He hides himself in an obscure angle of the porch.*
Oh, my mistress! Oh, Notre Dame!
Take my life! save my soul!

SCENE III.

QUASIMODO *hidden*, CLAUDE FROLLO, CLOPIN.

CLAUDE FROLLO.

So Phœbus is at Montfort?

CLOPIN.

My lord, he is not dead!

CLAUDE FROLLO

Provided nothing brings him here!

CLOPIN.

Do not fear it;
He is too feeble yet for such a journey.
If he came, 't would be his death.
My lord, you can feel sure
That every step would reopen his wound;
Do not fear anything this morning.

CLAUDE FROLLO.

Oh! let me hold her just to-day
For life or death within my power!
Hell! I'll give you all the rest,
If you grant me this one hour!
[*To* CLOPIN.]   They will soon bring the gypsy here!
You remember everything!
In the square — with your men —

CLOPIN.

Yes.

CLAUDE FROLLO.

Keep in the shadow;
If I cry, "To me!" you come.

CLOPIN.

Yes!

CLAUDE FROLLO.

Have plenty with you!

CLOPIN.

If you cry, "To me!"

CLAUDE FROLLO.

Yes.

CLOPIN.

I rush to her,
I tear her from the King's men —

CLAUDE FROLLO.

Yes.

CLOPIN.

And give her to you.

CLAUDE FROLLO.

Go, mix among the crowd,
  And perhaps she
Will look upon the priest
  More tenderly;
Then rush,—rush all of you—

CLOPIN.

      Yes, my master!

CLAUDE FROLLO.

Hold yourselves close!

CLOPIN.

      Yes.

CLAUDE FROLLO.

Hide your arms,
Not to excite suspicion!

CLOPIN.

      Master, you shall see!

CLAUDE FROLLO.

But hell may take her quick,
  With my good-will,
If now this insane creature
  Refuses still!

Destiny! Oh, fatal stroke!
  Friend, I count on thee!
On this my only chance I wait
  With fierce anxiety.

CLOPIN.

Fear nothing terrible, my lord,
  Count faithfully on me.

And on this last and only chance
Rely courageously!

[*They go out hurriedly. The populace begin to enter the square.*

SCENE IV.

The populace; QUASIMODO; *afterward* ESMERALDA, *and her escort; then* CLAUDE FROLLO, PHŒBUS, CLOPIN FROUILLEFOU, *priests, archers, officers of the law.*

CHORUS.

To Notre Dame
  Come, get a sight
Of the young woman
  Who dies to-night!

This gypsy woman
  Who stabbed, they say,
The handsomest officer
  In the King's pay.

In vain did Heaven
  Beauty lend her!
Is it possible —
  God defend her! —
A soul so black,
  An eye so tender!

A frightful thing,
  Human nature is so!
The poor unfortunate!
  Come, let us go

To Notre Dame
To get a sight
Of the young woman
Who dies to-night!

[*The crowd increases; noise; a gloomy procession begins to appear on the Place du Parvis. Rows of black penitents. Banners of La Miséricorde. Torches, archers, officers of the law and the watch. The soldiers disperse the crowd.* ESMERALDA *appears. She wears a chemise; a rope is around her neck; her feet are bare, and she is covered with a long black veil of crape. Following her, come the executioners and the King's officers. As the prisoner reaches the front of the church, a sombre chant is heard in the distance, coming from the interior of the church, whose doors are closed.*

CHORUS (*in the church*).

Omnes fluctus fluminis
Transierunt super me
In imo voraginis
Ubi plorant animæ.

[*The chant draws nearer. It bursts forth, at length, when near the doors, which open suddenly and discover the interior of the church. It is filled with a long procession of priests in their robes of ceremony; banners are borne before them.* CLAUDE FROLLO, *in sacerdotal costume, leads the procession. He goes toward the criminal.*

THE PEOPLE.

Alive to-day, to-morrow dead!
Heaven! thy wings around her spread!

ESMERALDA.

It is Phœbus who calls me
Unto our home eternal.

Where God will hold us in his arms,
   Safe from misfortunes cruel.
Though plunged in the abyss of woe,
   A joyful hope is given:
I am to die upon the earth
   To be re-born in heaven!

CLAUDE FROLLO.

To die so young, so beautiful!
   Alas! the guilty priest
Must suffer greater woe than she;
   He ne'er will be released.
Oh, hapless child of sorrow,
   Lost through my infamy,
You only die from off this earth,
   While heaven is lost to me!

THE PEOPLE

Alas! she is an infidel.
   God's words, unto us spoken,
Say that in heaven for such as she
   No blessed gate shall open.
Death holds her fast, what misery!
   She can escape it, never!
She dies unto the world this day,
   And unto heaven forever!

[*The procession approaches.* CLAUDE *accosts* ESMERALDA

ESMERALDA (*frozen with terror*).
It is the priest!
        CLAUDE FROLLO (*low*).
Yes, it is I! I love you, I entreat you!
Say but one word! 'T is not too late;
I can yet save you!
Say, I love you!

ESMERALDA.
I abhor you! Go!

CLAUDE FROLLO.
Then die! I'll go where I can find you!
[CLAUDE *turns to the crowd.*
We deliver this woman to the secular arm;
At this solemn moment may the breath of the Lord
Pass over her soul!
[*As the officers of the law are about to seize* ESMERALDA, QUASIMODO *jumps into the square, thrusts back the archers, takes* ESMERALDA *in his arms, and throws himself with her into the church.*

QUASIMODO.
Sanctuary! sanctuary! sanctuary!

THE PEOPLE.
Sanctuary! sanctuary! sanctuary!
Rejoice, O people!
Hail to the good bell-ringer!
  Oh, destiny!
  The criminal
  Belongs to heaven!
  The scaffold falls!
  The eternal God
  Instead of a tomb
  Discloses the altar!
  Executioners, back!
  King's officers, back!
  This barrier
  Limits your power.
  Thou hast changed
  Everything here.

The angels claim her;
She belongs to God!

CLAUDE FROLLO (*commanding silence by a gesture*).
She is not saved! She is a gypsy!
Notre Dame can save none but Christians!
Pagans are proscribed even when clasping the altar!
[*To the King's men.*] In the name of my lord the Archbishop of Paris,
I give you back this sinful woman!

QUASIMODO (*to the archers*).
I will defend her! I swear it.
Approach us not!

CLAUDE FROLLO (*to the archers*).
Do you hesitate?
Obey me, on the instant!
Tear the gypsy from this holy place.
[*The archers advance.* QUASIMODO *places himself between them and* ESMERALDA.

QUASIMODO
Never! [*A horseman is heard approaching. He calls out*:
Wait! [*The crowd disperses.*

PHŒBUS (*appearing on horseback. He is pale, breathless, exhausted as is a man who has made a long journey*).
Wait!

ESMERALDA.
Phœbus!

CLAUDE FROLLO (*aside, terrified*).
My plot has failed.

PHŒBUS *(leaping from his horse)*.

God be praised! I breathe
And I arrive in time!
This girl is innocent.
Behold my assassin!   [*Points to* CLAUDE FROLLO

ALL.

Heavens! the priest!

PHŒBUS.

The priest alone is guilty, and I will prove it!
Arrest him!

THE PEOPLE.

Oh, wonder!
    [*The archers surround* CLAUDE FROLLO

CLAUDE FROLLO.

God alone is Master!

ESMERALDA.

Phœbus!

PHŒBUS.

Esmeralda!
    [*They fall into each other's arms*

ESMERALDA.

My adored Phœbus, we shall live!

PHŒBUS.

Thou shalt live!

ESMERALDA.

For us shines happiness!

THE PEOPLE.

Live, both of you!

ESMERALDA.

Hear these joyous shouts!
At thy feet receive me, humble girl!
Heavens! thou art pale! What is the matter?

PHŒBUS (*staggering*).

I die!
[*She catches him in her arms. Expectation and anxiety among the crowd.*
Each step I took toward you, my beloved,
Reopened my wound, that was hardly healed.
I have taken your grave and given you life.
I die! Destiny has avenged thee.
My angel, I go to see
If heaven is worth thy love!
Farewell! [*He dies.*

ESMERALDA.

Phœbus! He dies! In an instant everything is changed!
[*She falls upon his body.*
I follow you into eternity.

CLAUDE FROLLO.

Fatality!

THE PEOPLE.
Fatality!

THE END.

www.ingramcontent.com/pod-product-compliance
Lightning Source LLC
Chambersburg PA
CBHW021319110426
42743CB00049B/3409